SELF-WORKING
COIN MAGIC
92 Foolproof Tricks

by Karl Fulves

With 251 Illustrations by
Joseph K. Schmidt

DOVER PUBLICATIONS, INC.
New York

Published in Canada by General Publishing Company, Ltd., 30 Lesmill Road, Don Mills, Toronto, Ontario.

Self-Working Coin Magic: 92 Foolproof Tricks is a new work, first published by Dover Publications, Inc., in 1989.

Manufactured in the United States of America
Dover Publications, Inc., 31 East 2nd Street, Mineola, N.Y. 11501

Library of Congress Cataloging-in-Publication Data

Fulves, Karl.
    Self-working coin magic : 92 foolproof tricks / by Karl Fulves ; with 251 illustrations by Joseph K. Schmidt.
        p.   cm.
    ISBN 0-486-26179-4
    1. Coin tricks. I. Schmidt, Joseph K. II. Title.
GV1599.F83   1989
793.8—dc20
                                                    89-36962
                                                        CIP

INTRODUCTION

"It would be difficult to overrate the importance of a good repertoire of well-rehearsed pocket tricks." Those words, written by Will Goldston, are as true today as when they first appeared more than a half century ago.

Pocket tricks are so called because they are performed with apparatus carried in the pocket. Routines with coins and bills are fundamental to pocket tricks. The magician who has mastered money magic will find it easy to apply his knowledge to many areas of close-up prestidigitation.

People are interested in money. The gyrations of the stock market are a topic of everyday conversation. Banks and investment houses advertise in daily newspapers. Television devotes nightly segments to money news. The magician who can perform a few tricks with coins and bills will have no trouble holding the attention of his audience. Current news stories about money matters suggest new and fresh ideas for presentation. Tie in a money trick to a story in the headlines and you will create immediate interest in the feat about to be performed.

Ingenious magical thinkers have developed a wide range of vivid magical effects with money: A trick like "Quick Print" (No. 5) allows you apparently to print a genuine $5 bill on blank paper; "Bunco Bills" (No. 70) takes the audience behind the scenes to expose the methods of the shortchange artist; "The Miser's Dream" (No. 87) fulfills the dream of seemingly plucking money from thin air.

In some tricks it is required that paper money be cut or otherwise altered. It is a federal law that U.S. currency cannot be defaced. For tricks in which money is altered, use realistic play money of the kind available in toy and novelty stores.

It should be noted that, although the directions given here seem to imply that the magician is a man (the traditional manner for giving directions in magic), they are, of course, also intended to be used by women.

To help readers outside the United States perform the tricks described in this book, the following diagram indicates the size of the coins used. U.S. paper bills (of all denominations) measure $2\frac{5}{8}'' \times 6\frac{3}{16}''$ (6.6 × 15.5 cm).

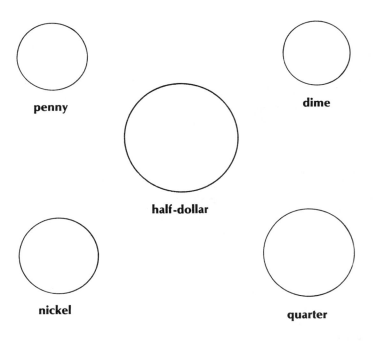

penny

dime

half-dollar

nickel

quarter

For their generous assistance in the preparation of this book I would like to thank Howard Wurst, Jo Sarles, Sam Schwartz and artist Joseph K. Schmidt.

KARL FULVES

Second
finger

Third
finger

First
finger

Fourth
finger

Thumb

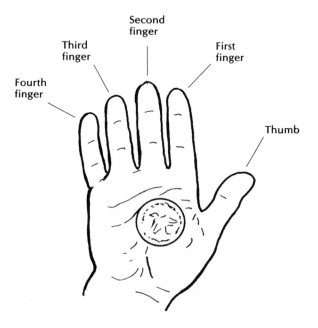

Fingers of the hand, as referred to in the text

CONTENTS

HAUNTED HOUSE   113

PLATFORM TRICKS   127

EASY MONEY MAGIC

Coin magic can be classified in the category of small magic, that is, magic performed with small objects. The best way to learn coin magic is to begin by performing simple tricks like those described in this chapter.

As with the handling of all small apparatus, take care to display coins or bills so they are clearly visible to the audience. The tricks in this chapter will acquaint you with basic ways of handling coins and bills. At the same time, the effects produce strong visual magic.

1. QUARTER BET

The magician displays a quarter on his left palm. He covers it with a half-dollar.

The magician says, "I'll bet you 15 cents you can't tell me whether the coin under the half-dollar is heads up or tails up. If you win, you keep the coin under the half-dollar."

Even if the spectator guesses correctly, he will be surprised, because when the half-dollar is lifted, the coin under it has changed to a dime.

Method: When you remove a handful of change from your left trouser pocket, place a quarter over a dime. Do not call attention to what you do. Place a half-dollar aside. Then pick up the remaining change (all except the quarter and the dime) and place this change in your right trouser pocket.

Fig. 1

Display the coins as shown in Figure 1. The right hand holds the half-dollar. The quarter is on the left palm. Unknown to the audience, there is a dime hidden under the quarter. Make some remark that calls attention to the quarter. You can say, for example, "I found this quarter just this morning. Let's see if it's lucky for me."

Place the half-dollar on top of the quarter. Tell the spectator that if he's willing to bet 15 cents, you will bet that he cannot guess whether the quarter is heads up or tails up. If he guesses correctly, you will give him the coin under the half-dollar.

Let him guess. If he guesses wrong, give him another chance. Then lift the half-dollar with the quarter under it. Place these two coins in the right pocket. From the spectator's point of view, a magical change has taken place—the quarter has changed to a dime.

2.   MONEY CHANGER

A dime is displayed at the right fingertips. Except for the coin, the hands are unmistakably empty. Rubbing the dime, the magician explains that friction produces heat and heat causes metal to expand.

When the dime is next shown, it has changed to a half-dollar.

Method: Beforehand, clip a half-dollar between the right first and second fingers, Figure 2. Then grip a dime as shown in Figure 3. The preparation can be done with the hand in the jacket pocket. The key to the working of this trick is that if the dime is pointed directly at the spectator, the half-dollar cannot be seen.

Display the dime as shown in Figure 3 by pointing it at the spectator. The hand appears to be empty. Bring the left hand in front of the coin. With the back of the left hand screening the action

Fig. 2   **Fig. 3**

from audience view, silently pivot the dime around onto the half-dollar with the left thumb, Figure 4.

Rub the coin. Then display the half-dollar. The dime is hidden behind the larger coin. From the audience's view, the dime has magically changed to a much larger coin. It is a startling transformation.

There is a little-known variation. Clip two half-dollars one behind the other, as shown in Figure 2. Place a dime in front of them and display the dime as shown in Figure 3.

Perform the handling shown in Figure 4 to pivot the dime around onto the upper half-dollar. Turn the hands so the back of the right hand is toward the audience.

Lift the upper half-dollar with the left hand and display it, Figure 5. The dime is concealed behind this half-dollar. Say, "Some people think I have two coins. I do." Now bring the other half-dollar into view with the right hand.

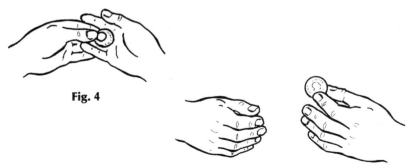

Fig. 4

Fig. 5

3. FIVE RISER

A $1 bill is placed on top of a $5 bill as shown in Figure 6. Starting at the bottom edge, both bills are rolled together, Figure 7. When the $5 bill has been completely rolled into a cylinder, Figure 8, the magician stops and has the spectator place his finger on the $1 bill to prevent trickery.

The bills are unrolled, but now the $5 bill is on top of the $1 bill.

Method: This adaptation of a classic trick with napkins or handkerchiefs was suggested by Monty Crowe. Place the $1 bill on top of the $5 bill as shown in Figure 6. Point out that the $1 bill is on top of the $5 bill.

Roll the two bills together as shown in Figure 7. Continue rolling the two bills until the $5 bill has been rolled into a cylinder, Figure 8. If you continue rolling the two bills the edge of the $5 bill will flip over.

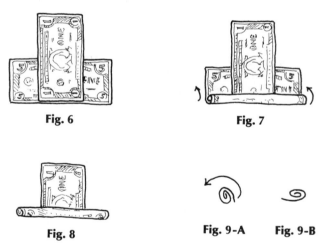

Fig. 6   Fig. 7

Fig. 8   Fig. 9-A   Fig. 9-B

This flip-over action is shown in the end view of Figures 9-A and 9-B. When the long edge of the $5 bill reaches the position shown in Figure 9-B, stop rolling the bills. Have the spectator place his finger on the $1 bill to prevent trickery.

Slowly unroll the bills. The $5 bill will be on top of the $1 bill as shown in Figure 10.

Fig. 10

4. ONE FROM TWO

The magician displays two coins, showing them front and back. Openly placing one coin in his pocket, he snaps his fingers and opens his hand. Both coins are back in the hand.

Method: E. G. Ervin invented the principle behind this trick. Arrange three coins as shown in Figure 11. The coins do not have to be identical. Coins *A* and *C* can be half-dollars, coin *B* a quarter. Make sure the coins are arranged with heads showing the same way on all coins.

With the coins so arranged, place them between the thumb and first finger, at the base of the thumb, as shown in Figure 12. When the coins are in this position they can be shown on both sides. It appears as if you hold two coins.

Grasp the coins with the left hand to hold them in place, Figure 13. Then close the right hand around the coins. Remove either coin

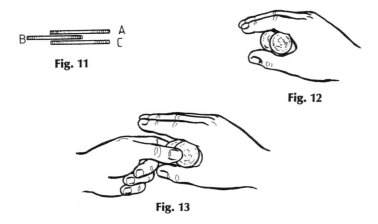

Fig. 11

Fig. 12

Fig. 13

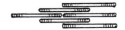

Fig. 14

A or coin *C*, show it and place it in the pocket. Snap the fingers. Wait a second, shake your head as if something went wrong, then snap the fingers again.

Open the hand to show that the second coin has apparently returned.

An arrangement suggested by Ervin for six coins is shown in Figure 14. With the coins held as shown in Figure 12, three coins will show. Close the hand around the coins as before. Remove and pocket three coins. Snap the fingers and all three coins seem to have returned to the right hand.

5. QUICK PRINT

Several dollar-size pieces of blank paper are shown. They are folded and dropped into a paper cup. One is removed. The magician passes his hand over it. The blank paper changes to a $5 bill. There is no switch of paper.

Method: The trick depends on the little-noticed fact that a crisp new $5 bill contains an unprinted white area. The $5 bill is held so the side with the Lincoln Memorial is uppermost. The white area surrounds the Memorial, Figure 15.

Fold the bill as shown in Figure 16 to bring the white area to the center. Then fold the green portion at the top, bottom and sides around in back. The result will be that only the white shows, Figure 17. Place this folded $5 bill in the paper cup along with several dollar-size pieces of white paper.

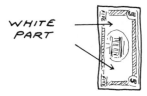

WHITE PART

Fig. 15

Fig. 16

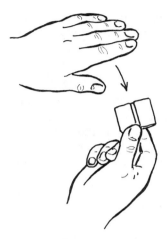

Fig. 17

When presenting the routine, remove a piece of blank paper, show both sides and fold it as described above. Drop it into the cup.

Do the same thing with the other pieces of paper. As you do, remark that a fellow once showed you a simple way to print money from blank paper. Shake up the contents of the cup. Then reach in and remove the folded $5 bill.

Bring it out so the audience sees the white surface. The bill looks like a blank piece of paper. Hold the bill between the right thumb and first finger.

Pass the left hand over the bill, Figure 17. As you do, allow the bill to turn over. This brings the inked surface into view. Open the bill to show that a blank piece of paper apparently changed into a crisp new $5 bill.

6. QUICK COPPER

The old British pennies used before that currency converted to the decimal system are coins almost the same size as American half-dollars. They are obtainable in shops that sell foreign coins. A combination of English pennies and American half-dollars is used in a quick trick devised by Sam Aaronson.

The magician stacks four English pennies and four half-dollars so they alternate penny, half, penny, half, etc.

Four of the coins are tossed into the opposite hand. When the hand is opened, it contains four half-dollars. The halves have instantly separated themselves from the English coins.

Method: Although English pennies appear to be the same size as American half-dollars, they are slightly larger. This small difference in size is exploited in the following handling.

Stack four English pennies and four American half-dollars so they alternate. Then grasp the stack from above with the right hand, Figure 18.

Say, "Let's mix the coins a bit more." Make a tossing motion toward the left hand. Gently release the pressure of the right fingers. This will cause the smaller half-dollars to slip out of the right fingers and into the left hand, Figure 19. The back of the right hand is toward the audience, so the spectators cannot see which coins are being tossed into the left hand.

Immediately, close both hands into loose fists. Shake the coins a bit. Say, "This is a quick way to extract copper from silver." Open the hands one at a time to show that copper has separated from silver. The trick can also be done with four American nickels and four American pennies.

Another way to do the trick is to hand the eight coins to a spectator. Have him cup them between his hands and shake them

Fig. 18

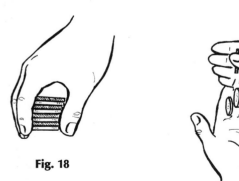

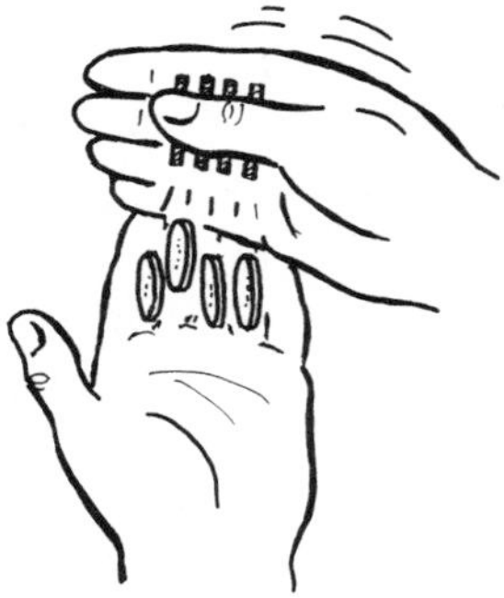

Fig. 19

up. With the coins randomly mixed, hold them as shown in Figure 18. Then go through the above handling to cause the randomly mixed coins to separate into copper and silver.

7. ANIMATION

This is a gag that will amuse some and mystify others. The magician wraps six copper pennies and a silver coin in a handkerchief. He says, "The silver coin doesn't like to be among copper coins. In a second you'll see it try to jump out of the handkerchief."

Several seconds go by. Nothing happens. The magician says, "The silver coin dislikes salt even more. I'll go to the kitchen and sprinkle salt on the silver coin. Then you'll see it move."

The magician starts to leave for the kitchen with the handkerchief-wrapped coins. Immediately, the silver coin begins gyrating wildly inside the handkerchief.

Method: The secret is simple. Just as you reach the doorway, pause with the handkerchief bag at the edge of the doorway in view of the audience. The other arm is behind the other side of the doorway. Bend it back, allowing the fingers to snap against the handkerchief bag, Figure 20.

The result is that the handkerchief bag will begin to gyrate as if the coins inside have sprung to life. Do this for just a second. Say, "The silver coin doesn't want me even to mention salt." Step back into the room and continue with further mysteries.

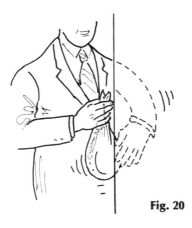

Fig. 20

8. NEVER WAS

While the magician turns his head aside, a spectator places a coin on the magician's outstretched palm. The coin is covered with a handkerchief. "I'm going to try to guess the date on the coin," the magician says.

He thinks psychic thoughts, then says, "I get the date 2001, a date that doesn't exist yet. That means the coin doesn't exist." Removing the handkerchief, he shows that the coin has vanished.

Method: This coin vanish is a favorite of Tony Kardyro. The only requirement is that you wear a watch.

Turn your head to one side and have a coin placed on the left palm. Keep the head turned away as you begin to cover the coin with a handkerchief.

The corner of the handkerchief is held between the right first and second fingers. As the handkerchief is drawn over the coin, the coin is clipped between the thumb and first finger, Figure 21. The handkerchief hides the steal.

As the handkerchief is drawn farther over the left palm, the coin is slipped under the wristwatch as shown in Figure 21.

At this point, announce that you will try to guess the date on the coin. Look skyward, then announce that the date is 2001 or some such future date. Say, "That means the coin doesn't exist yet." Whisk away the handkerchief to reveal that the coin has vanished.

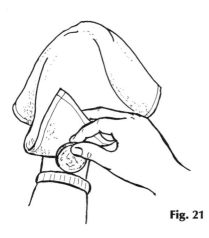

Fig. 21

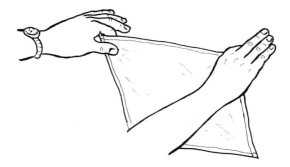

Fig. 22

If you are wearing a jacket, the jacket sleeve will keep the coin concealed from audience view. If you are performing the trick in a short-sleeved shirt, keep the left hand behind the handkerchief when showing that the coin has vanished, Figure 22.

If you want added cover for the coin, prepare by turning the watch face to the inside of the wrist. Then the coin can be slipped under the watch face rather than under the band. Most watch faces are large enough to cover the coin completely.

When you have completed the vanish of the coin, the spectator is likely to say that *your* coin might not exist but *his* does. Reply, "Actually, your coin has gone through a time warp. It was transported here." Remove from the pocket a coin of the same value and hand it to the spectator.

STAND-UP MAGIC

Amateur and professional magicians agree on the value of good stand-up tricks for their acts. Tricks that are performed while standing can be seen by the maximum number of spectators. Also, such tricks require nothing in the way of tables or special settings. Armed with nothing more than a few simple props, the stand-up magician can step before the audience and immediately proceed to perform miracles.

Almost all of the tricks in this chapter use props that may be borrowed. Some, like "Penny-tration" (No. 11), can be done close up. Others, like "Hot Silver" (No. 14), are ideal for platform or stage acts.

9. SLAP COIN

Bob Hummer invented a quick trick that produces startling visual magic. The magician places a coin in the left hand. The left hand is closed into a fist.

The right hand is slapped on top of the left fist. When the right hand is lifted, the coin is on top of the left fist, Figure 23, having apparently penetrated the fist.

Method: Flip a coin in the air and catch it in the left palm. Close the left hand into a loose fist and turn the left hand palm down.

Slap the top of the left fist with the right hand, Figure 24. As you do, move both hands up. At the same time release the coin.

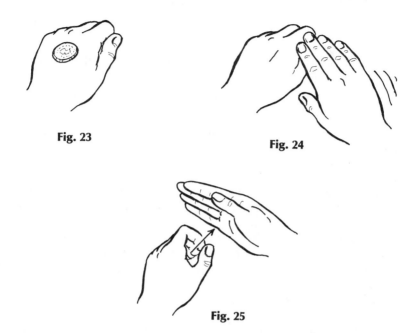

Fig. 23

Fig. 24

Fig. 25

The coin will sail out of the left fist as shown by the arrow in the exposed view in Figure 25. It will bounce off the right palm and come to rest on top of the left hand.

There is a knack to making the motion. The left hand should move up and stop abruptly. Allow the coin to keep moving so it sails out of the left hand, ricochets off the right palm and comes to rest on top of the left fist. All that remains is to lift the right hand away to show that the coin has apparently penetrated the left hand.

Practice the motion so it is imperceptible. When you have mastered it, you may wish to try a variation suggested by Bruce Elliott. Drop a handful of change into the left hand. Close the hand into a fist. Keep jingling the coins. As the right hand moves to a position over the left fist, Figure 24, the motion of the left hand is used to work the coins to a position near the opening in the fist.

Use the maneuver shown in Figure 25 to propel the coins out of the fist, against the right palm and onto the top of the left fist. Freeze the hands. Then slowly draw the right hand away to show the coins on top of the left hand.

10. MONEY MAKES MONEY

"You've heard the saying that money makes money," the magician says. "Let me show you what that means."

He displays a dollar bill, folds it, snaps his fingers and causes a half-dollar to materialize from within the bill.

Method: Have the bill and a half-dollar in the pocket. Reach into the pocket, place the coin behind the bill, then remove the apparatus so the bill faces the audience with the coin concealed in back.

Snap the left side of the bill with the left fingers, Figure 26. This shows the left hand empty and also indicates that the left side of the bill does not conceal a coin.

Grasp the left side of the bill with the left hand. Then transfer the coin from the right to the left hand as shown in Figure 27. This clever move was invented by Clayton Rosencrance.

When the coin has been secretly transferred to a position under the left thumb, snap the right side of the bill with the right first finger, Figure 28.

Fold the bill into quarters with the coin inside. Then tilt the folded bill downward so the coin slowly emerges from inside the bill, Figure 29.

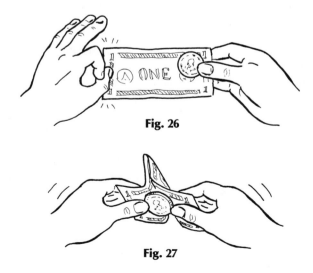

Fig. 26

Fig. 27

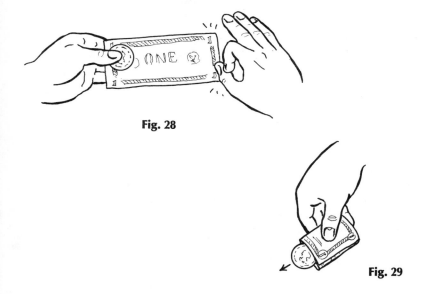

Fig. 28

Fig. 29

11.   PENNY-TRATION

A spectator is given seven pennies to hold. The magician causes one penny to penetrate the spectator's hand. This fine trick was invented by Harry Baker.

Method: The seven pennies can be borrowed. There are no extra pennies and no gimmicks. The trick depends on timing for its success.

Hold the pennies cupped in the left hand. Stand facing the spectator. Have him hold his right hand palm up. Pour the pennies into his hand. Have him count them one at a time back into your hand. He should count them aloud. This impresses on the spectator's mind that there are exactly seven pennies.

Again, have the spectator hold his hand palm up. Explain that you are going to count the pennies into his hand one at a time, and that when you have counted the seventh coin, he is to clench his hand into a tight fist quickly to trap the coins.

Use your right hand to pick up the first coin. Place it into the

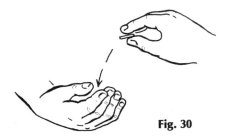

Fig. 30

spectator's hand on the count of one, Figure 30. After you have placed the first coin in his hand, allow each succeeding coin to click against a coin in the spectator's hand.

After five pennies have been placed in the spectator's hand, his eyes and ears are conditioned by the motion and sound. When you pick up the sixth coin, simply click it against a coin in the spectator's hand. Do not let go of it. Click it against one of the coins in his hand and bring the coin right back out again, still gripped between the right thumb and first finger. Keep the back of the hand toward the spectator to conceal the penny from view.

The last penny is tossed from your left hand into the spectator's hand. He closes his fist. Keep the back of the right hand to the spectator. Bring the right hand under the spectator's closed hand. Slap your hand against the back of his hand. Then bring your hand out, showing the penny. It appears that one penny penetrated his hand.

12.   IMPROMPTU BILL VANISH

A borrowed $5 bill is rolled up and placed into the spectator's hand. When he opens his hand, the bill has vanished. It is found in the magician's pocket.

Method: Tightly roll a borrowed $5 bill into a cylinder. Stand so the spectator is on your left. Hold the bill in the right hand. The edge of the bill contacts the first finger. This keeps the bill from unraveling.

Have the spectator hold his right hand palm up. Grasp his right wrist with your left hand.

Raise the bill in the direction of the arrow in Figure 31. Then

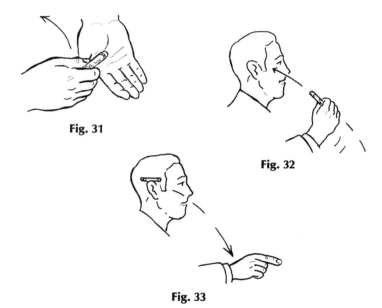

Fig. 31

Fig. 32

Fig. 33

bring it down so it strikes the spectator's palm. Instruct him that on the count of three he is to close his hand quickly around the bill.

Swing your hand in an arc, first up, then down so the bill strikes the spectator's palm. Count "one" as the bill hits his palm. Repeat the move and count "two" as the bill again hits the spectator's palm. Each time move the hand in an upward arc using a relaxed motion. The hand goes to the right of the face as shown in Figure 32.

As you perform the motion the third time, bring the bill up to the ear and leave the bill behind the ear, Figure 33.

Without hesitating, bring the right hand down. The extended first finger strikes the spectator's palm as shown in Figure 33. The spectator closes his hand around your finger.

Move your fingers in the direction of the spectator's jacket sleeve as if tossing the bill into the sleeve. The spectator opens his hand and discovers the bill is gone. He will probably look in his sleeve for the missing money. This trick was suggested by Gaylord Hill.

You can turn to your right and retrieve the bill from behind the ear. Another approach is to have a duplicate $5 bill rolled in a cylinder and kept in the pocket. Produce this bill and hand it back to the spectator.

13.   CRASH GLASS

A borrowed coin is tapped against the bottom of a borrowed glass. The coin visibly penetrates the glass and ends up inside the glass.

Method: This amazing trick was devised by the Canadian magician Ross Bertram. Hold the glass in the left hand. The mouth of the glass is against the palm. The glass is gripped by the thumb and little finger. The remaining fingers can be moved without disturbing the grip on the glass.

Borrow a coin. Take it with the right hand. Tap it against the bottom of the glass, Figure 34.

Separate the hands. The hands are then brought together in a quick motion. Unknown to the audience, the coin is thrown so it is caught by the extended left fingers, Figure 35. The right hand should be slightly in front of the left. The coin will travel in front of the glass.

As soon as the coin is caught, move the left hand sharply to the left, then back to the right. In this action the coin is allowed to enter

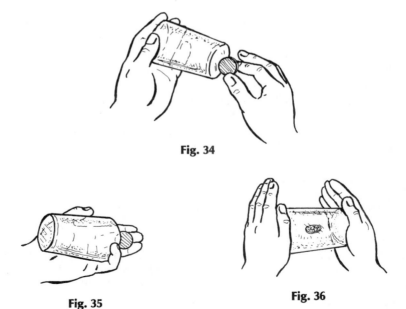

Fig. 34

Fig. 35

Fig. 36

the glass. The right palm contacts the bottom of the glass. The result is the situation shown in Figure 36. When the trick is properly performed, the coin travels too quickly for it to be followed by the eye.

14. HOT SILVER

Needed are two handkerchiefs, a paper bag and a borrowed coin. One handkerchief is folded and placed in the paper bag. The borrowed coin is marked and placed inside the other handkerchief. It vanishes at the snap of the fingers.

The magician reaches into the paper bag, removes the other handkerchief, gives it a shake and the coin tumbles into view.

This beautiful routine stems from ideas of John V. Hope and Robert Olsen.

Method: The handkerchiefs may be kept folded in the paper bag until you are ready to perform the routine. Have the spectator remove the handkerchiefs, unfold them and hand one to you. This indicates to the audience that there are no gimmicks or extra coins.

Borrow a coin and have it marked. While this is done, have the spectator fold his handkerchief and return it to the bag.

Drape the other handkerchief over the left hand. Grasp the coin through the fabric. Display it as shown in Figure 37. The left side should be toward the audience.

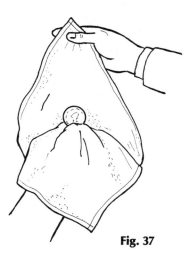

Fig. 37

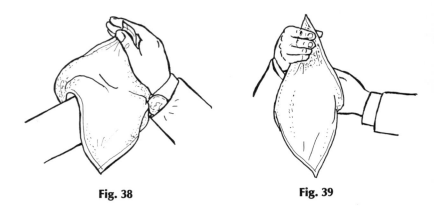

Fig. 38   **Fig. 39**

As the right hand drapes the handkerchief over the coin, the right jacket sleeve moves to a position near the coin. With no change in pace, drop the coin into the right sleeve, Figure 38. The back of the left hand should be toward the audience at this point. The handkerchief covers the sleeving of the coin as shown in the audience's view, Figure 39.

When the end of the handkerchief has been draped over the left hand, release the right hand. Then grasp the center of the handkerchief with the right hand, as if grasping the coin through the fabric. Bring the left hand out from under the handkerchief and grasp the center of the handkerchief.

Raise the right hand. The palm of the right hand should be toward the audience with the fingers widespread to show the right hand unmistakably empty. Snap the right fingers.

Grasp one corner of the handkerchief with the right hand. Shake the handkerchief to show that the coin has vanished.

Pretend to drop the handkerchief to the floor accidentally. The next maneuver subtly demonstrates that the coin is not in the sleeve. When you raised the right hand to snap the fingers, the coin slid to a position near the elbow. Kneel to pick up the handkerchief, placing the elbow against the right knee, Figure 40.

With the elbow pressed against the knee, reach down with the right hand to take the handkerchief, Figure 41. The coin is trapped and cannot move. Reverse the above procedure as you stand up.

Hand the handkerchief to the spectator. Show both hands empty. Reach into the bag with the right hand. Allow the coin to slide out of the sleeve. Catch it with the right hand while the hand is inside the bag. If you miss the coin, it will fall noiselessly onto the folded handkerchief.

Grasp the coin with the curled fingers. Remove the handkerchief from the bag. Give the handkerchief a shake. Release the coin, allowing it to fall to the table. Let the spectator verify the mark.

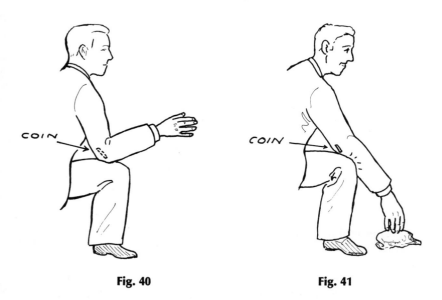

Fig. 40   Fig. 41

15.   AIR TRAFFIC

The magician places a coin in his hand and makes a fist. A pen or pencil is pushed through the fist, causing the coin to vanish. When the pen is pushed through the fist again, the coin reappears.

Method: Place the coin in the left hand, close the hand into a loose fist and turn the hand palm down.

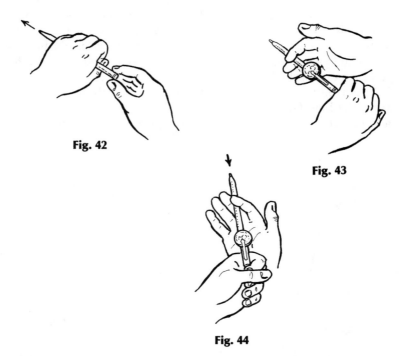

Fig. 42

Fig. 43

Fig. 44

The right hand picks up a pen that has a clip. The pen is pushed into the left fist, Figure 42, so that the coin is secretly engaged in the clip.

The pen is grasped between the first and second fingers of the right hand, Figure 43, and pulled out of the left hand. The back of the right hand screens the stolen coin from audience view.

Open the left hand to show that the coin has vanished. Then close the left hand into a fist. Push the pen into the fist, Figure 44, allowing the coin to slide free of the clip. Remove the pen and wave it over the left hand. Open the left hand to show that the coin has returned.

16.   HIGHER

The magician places a half-dollar in his eye as if the coin were a monocle. He turns slowly around. The coin has vanished. The magician retrieves the coin from the top of his head!

Fig. 45

Method: Hold the inside of the jacket handkerchief pocket open with a wadded piece of cloth. A small handkerchief may be used if it is not too bulky. When no one is looking, place a half-dollar on top of the head.

Remove another half-dollar from the pocket. Place it on the eye as if it were a monocle. Say something like, "Here's how I keep an eye on my money."

Turn around slowly. When your back is to the spectator, allow the coin to drop into the handkerchief pocket, Figure 45.

Continue turning until you face the audience again. Say, "Of course my money has a mind of its own." Slowly reach up to the top of the head and remove the duplicate coin.

MATTER THRU MATTER

Coin penetrations are considered among the most dramatic of magical effects. The tricks in this chapter are impromptu and represent outstanding creative thinking in magic.

17. DROP KICK

This beautifully simple method of causing a coin to penetrate a tabletop was devised by J. W. Sarles. As the audience sees it, four half-dollars are placed in a stack on the table. The stack is covered with an inverted cup. Instantly, one half-dollar penetrates the table.

Method: Stack four half-dollars on top of one another, overlapping so that each coin is slightly forward of the coin beneath it. Place an inverted coffee cup over the stack in such a way that the lip of the cup is brought down on top of the bottom coin of the stack. The situation is shown in Figure 46.

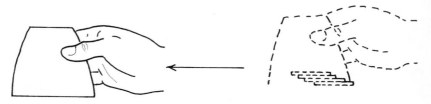

Fig. 46

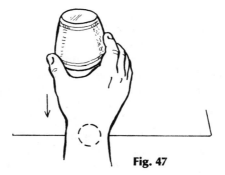

Fig. 47

Immediately, slide the stack forward to a point past the center of the table, in the direction of the arrow shown in Figure 46. As you do, the bottom coin will remain in place. The right wrist will conceal the coin from audience view.

The right wrist bears down on the half-dollar. The right hand then brings the cup back toward the near edge of the table in the direction of the arrow shown in Figure 47. The result is that the coin under the wrist slides back. Continue drawing the cup back until the concealed coin falls off the table and into the lap. The cup should be near the center of the table at this point.

Show the left hand empty. Then place the left hand under the table. Grasp the coin in the lap and tap it against the underside of the table.

Lift the cup with the right hand. There are only three coins. Bring the fourth coin into view and toss it onto the table.

If, when practicing, you find that the coin dropped into the lap tends to fall or roll to the floor, spread a napkin or handkerchief on the lap prior to presenting the routine.

18.   TIMING PATTERN

Two coins are repeatedly counted onto the table. One coin is placed under the table. The other coin magically penetrates the table to join the first coin.

Method: This trick, a favorite of Jacob Daley, demonstrates how timing and rhythm can convert a simple handling into a puzzling mystery.

Place a coin on the table and another in the palm-up left hand, Figure 48. The right hand picks up the coin from the table by sliding it off the near edge. At the same time the left hand turns palm down in the direction of the arrow shown in Figure 49.

The left hand slaps its coin onto the table. The other coin is held by the right thumb and first finger. The situation is shown in Figure 49.

The coin in the right hand is slapped onto the left palm, Figure 50. You are now back at the starting position. The timing should be such that you reach Figure 49 on the count of one and Figure 50 on the count of two. To put it another way, the left hand is slapped onto the table on the count of one, and the right hand is slapped onto the left palm for the count of two.

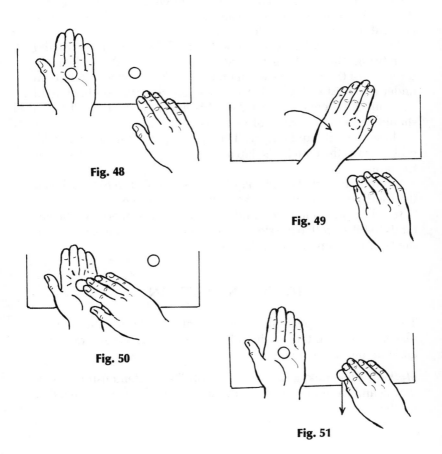

Fig. 48

Fig. 49

Fig. 50

Fig. 51

Repeat the above sequence several times. When you reach the position of Figure 50 the final time, begin to take the coin from the table with the right hand, but instead draw the coin off the table and allow it to drop into the lap, Figure 51.

Slap the left hand onto the table. Leave the coin there. Turn the left hand palm up. Slap the right hand onto the left palm as if slapping the coin onto the palm. The empty left palm then slaps the tabletop. The right hand draws the visible coin off the table and goes to the lap. Immediately the right hand picks up the coin in the lap.

The left hand is raised and turned palm up to show that the coin has vanished. The right hand then comes up into view with the two coins. Apparently one coin penetrated the tabletop.

19.   TUNNEL MOVE

The magician remarks that some tabletops have a built-in tunnel. He slaps a coin down on the table, slides it to the position directly over the invisible tunnel and causes the coin to penetrate the table.

Method: Unknown to the audience, two coins are used. One coin is concealed in the lap at the start. Display the duplicate coin on the left palm, then slap it down onto the table, Figure 52. The hand is about 10″–12″ from the near edge of the table.

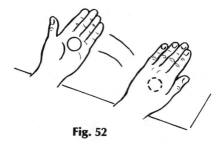

Fig. 52

Show the right hand empty and place it under the table. When the right hand is out of sight, allow it to take the coin from the lap. The right hand then moves to a position under the table that is directly below the left hand.

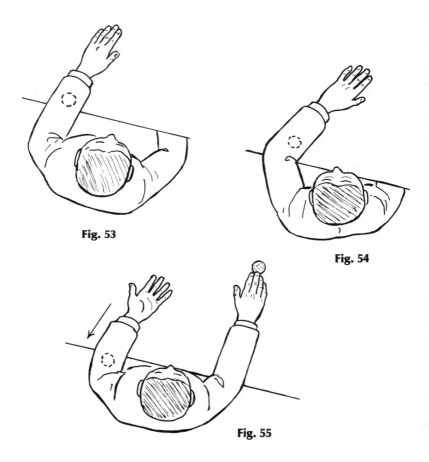

Fig. 53

Fig. 54

Fig. 55

The left hand pretends to slide its coin to the center of the table. Actually, the coin is left in place as the left hand moves outward. The coin is now under the left arm, Figure 53.

If the left hand really slid the coin out toward the center of the table, the coin would make a noise as it slid over the tabletop. Since there is no coin in the left hand, the sound must be simulated. This is accomplished in a subtle way. The right hand slides its coin along the underside of the table to create the sound.

When the left hand is at a point near the center of the table, slap it against the tabletop and spread the fingers, Figure 54. Immediately, bring the duplicate coin into view with the right hand.

Drop the visible coin onto the table. Then slide it back toward the body. At the same time draw the left arm back. The result is that the coin concealed under the left arm slides back and falls into the lap, Figure 55. The right hand can then toss the visible coin into the left, thus showing in an indirect way that only one coin has been used.

The above effect is based on a brilliant routine invented by Slydini.

20.   GLASS GO

"A magician from Tibet taught me two tricks," the magician says. He places a newspaper-wrapped glass over two coins. "The first trick was a way to cause a coin to disappear." The magician lifts the glass. The coins are still there.

He covers the coins again with the glass. When he lifts the glass, one coin has vanished, but it is obvious the coin is hidden under the other coin.

"The other trick was better," the magician says. "He taught me how to push a glass through the table." The magician slaps his hand on top of the newspaper covering the glass. The paper crumples. The glass has been pushed right through the table.

Method: This trick is a classic of misdirection. Wrap the glass with newspaper. Place the wrapped glass over a dime and a quarter, Figure 56. The coins rest on the table about 12" from the near edge.

Lift the wrapped glass away from the coins by bringing the glass back toward the near edge of the table. Let the audience see that nothing has happened.

Fig. 56

Bring the wrapped glass in front of the coins to screen them from audience view. Place the quarter on top of the dime, then cover the coins with the glass.

Remark that mind waves are needed to vanish the dime. Lift the glass and bring it to the near edge of the table. As the audience gazes at the coin, release pressure, allowing the glass to slide out of the paper and into the waiting right hand, Figure 57.

The audience is sure to deduce that the dime "vanished" by the obvious expedient of concealing it under the quarter. Cover the coins with the newspaper. Because the newspaper retains its shape, the audience thinks the glass is still under the newspaper.

Say, "The *other* trick was a better one. He taught me how to push a solid glass through the table." Smash the newspaper down flat on the table. Bring the glass into view with the other hand.

The author has sometimes used a version with a different outcome. After failing two or three times to get one coin to vanish, the magician says, "If I try this long enough, I'll need a cup of coffee to stay awake." He taps the paper cover, then lifts it away, revealing that the glass has changed to a coffee cup.

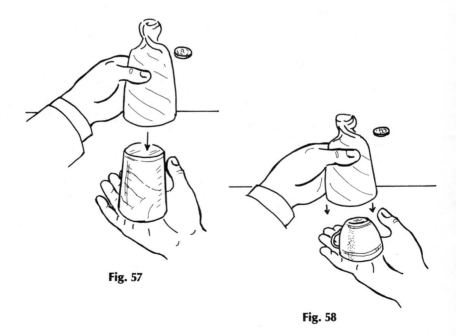

Fig. 57

Fig. 58

The coffee cup is in the lap at the start. The coins are covered with the newspaper-wrapped glass. Bring the wrapped glass back to the edge of the table. While attention is on the coins, release the glass, allowing it to fall into the waiting right hand. Silently place the glass on the lap.

Cover the coins again. Recite a few mystic words. Lift the paper cover, bringing it to the near edge of the table. As you do, place it directly over the coffee cup, Figure 58. Place the paper-wrapped cup on top of the coins.

Tap the paper, then lift it away to reveal that the glass has apparently changed to a coffee cup.

In a similar way you can cause the glass to change to a smaller glass, a ball or other small object.

21.   RUB A DUB

The magician places a half-dollar on a cloth-covered table. He rubs the coin with a circular motion. The coin is rubbed right through the center of the table.

Method: Place a half-dollar on the table about 10″ from the near edge. The table should be covered with a tablecloth. Cover the coin with the left hand, Figure 59.

Move the hand forward, beginning a circular motion as indicated by the arrow in Figure 59. But as the hand moves forward, it lifts slightly away from the coin, leaving the coin on the table. When the hand reaches the center of the table, the coin is concealed under the wrist, Figure 60.

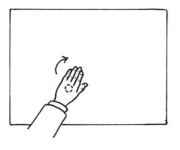

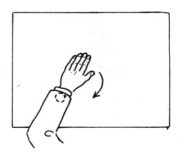

Fig. 59   **Fig. 60**

Bring the hand back, continuing the circular motion as indicated by the arrow shown in Figure 60. But this time, bear down on the coin so that as the hand moves back toward the near edge of the table, the coin slides back also.

Proceed in a similar manner, leaving the coin in place as the hand moves forward, drawing it back as the hand moves back toward the near edge of the table. After two such circular sweeps, the coin will have secretly shifted to a position at the near edge of the table, Figure 61.

On the next sweep, allow the coin to fall silently into the lap. Then place the right hand in the lap, pick up the coin and bring the coin to the center of the table. Figure 62 shows the situation at this point. The coin is in the right hand. The audience thinks the coin is under the left hand.

Tap the left hand against the center of the table. At the same time, tap the coin up against the tabletop from below with the right hand. Synchronize the motions so it appears the tapping sound is made by the coin under the left palm.

Slap the left hand against the tabletop. Then lift it away to show that the coin has vanished. Bring the right hand out holding the coin.

Ross Bertram suggested for patter a line about using the circular rubbing motion to polish silver coins. After the left hand has been lifted to show the coin gone, the performer remarks, "Looks like I rubbed too hard."

Fig. 61   **Fig. 62**

J. W. Sarles did the Rub-a-Dub effect with two coins on a hard surface like a wooden-topped table. He placed two quarters on the table, then used the Rub-a-Dub method to cause one coin to be worked backward to fall into the lap. Sarles remarked as one coin apparently penetrated the table, "That's how you can tell a real coin from a counterfeit."

22.   WINGED SILVER

A coin is placed in a glass and covered with a handkerchief. On command, the coin leaves the glass and appears inside a ball of wool.

Method: The handling is based on an elegant coin vanish of Otto Waldmann's. Drop a quarter into a drinking glass. Place a handkerchief over the glass. The handkerchief is kept in place by snapping a rubber band over the apparatus. The rubber band should go around the glass at about the middle of the glass, Figure 63.

Fig. 63   **Fig. 64**

Lift the glass with the left hand. As you do, allow upward pressure of the hand to slide the handkerchief and rubber band up about an inch to the position shown in Figure 64. There is now some slack at the top. Make sure the rubber band holds the handkerchief snugly in place but not so tightly as to interfere with the upward motion of the handkerchief.

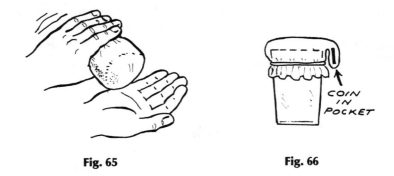

Fig. 65   **Fig. 66**

Shake the glass so the coin rattles around inside. Then tip the mouth of the glass toward the right hand, Figure 65. The coin inside will make a clinking sound. As soon as it does, close the right hand into a fist as if the coin was poured into the right hand.

Place the glass down. You will note the coin tipped out of the glass and now lies in a cloth bag made from the slack in the handkerchief. The situation is shown in Figure 66. The glass is placed on the table so the portion with the coin is away from the audience.

Show the left hand empty. Pick up a ball of wool from the table with the left hand. In the center of the ball of wool is a duplicate coin, placed there before the performance.

With the right hand, make a tossing motion toward the ball of wool. Open the right hand to show it empty. Then grasp the handkerchief with the right hand, secretly pinching the coin so it is held in place. Gently lift the handkerchief away from the glass. Place the handkerchief in the pocket.

Have a spectator hold the ball of wool in his cupped hands. Unravel the wool to reveal the coin.

COIN STUNTS

One way to bring attention to the subject of coin magic is to perform a few stunts with coins. When you have audience attention focused on the apparatus, it is an easy matter to perform tricks with the coins. This chapter is a collection of some of the best stunts and puzzles with coins.

23. STAY PUT

A coin is balanced on the first finger. The first finger is slapped against the palm of the other hand, yet the coin mysteriously remains balanced on the first finger. The feat cannot be duplicated unless the spectator knows the secret.

Fig. 67

Method: Balance a coin on the right first finger as shown in Figure 67. Hold the palm-up left hand under the right hand. The left fingers are curled upward.

Turn the right hand palm down. As you swing the right hand down toward the left palm, press the coin against the right thumb, Figure 68. The thumb and first finger bend back out of sight.

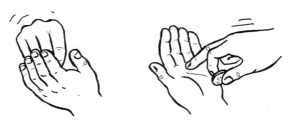

Fig. 68

The right second finger slaps against the left palm as shown in Figure 68.

As the right hand moves back to the position shown in Figure 67, the action is reversed. The first finger straightens, while the second finger curls inward.

Make sure the audience is in front of you. Keep the left fingers curled. As shown in the audience view of Figure 68, this helps conceal the action from the spectators.

Done three or four times in quick succession, the stunt produces the illusion that the coin is mysteriously stuck to the finger. Spectators unfamiliar with the secret will be unable to duplicate the feat.

24. FLIP OUT

The magician places a coin on his palm-up hand. The coin is tossed into the air. Curiously, it spins rapidly, as if it had been flipped by the thumb and finger.

Method: Rest the coin on the open palm. As the coin is tossed upward, allow the tip of the thumb to contact the edge of the coin. It is this action that imparts a spin to the coin.

There is a variation that is even more puzzling. Place a penny, a nickel and a dime on the open palm. The coins are some distance from one another, with the penny near the thumb, Figure 69.

Fig. 69

As you toss all three coins into the air, remark that the copper in the penny absorbs more heat than other coins and will act differently.

When you make the toss, allow the edge of the penny (and no other coin) to contact the thumb. This imparts a spin to the penny. When the coins are in the air, only the penny will be spinning.

25. THE PIVOT

Hold two quarters together between the thumb and second finger, Figure 70. The tip of the first finger contacts the edge of the front quarter, Figure 71, and pulls it up and over the other quarter. The front quarter, shown shaded in these drawings, ends up in back of the other quarter. The back quarter remains stationary throughout.

Once learned, the stunt can be repeated rapidly. Others who try the stunt will find it difficult to perform.

Method: To the audience, the trick looks as shown in the drawings. In fact it is impossible to perform that way because the back quarter will move or tip as soon as you attempt to pull the front quarter upward.

Fig. 70

Fig. 71

Fig. 72-A   **Fig. 72-B**

The secret is that the first finger contacts the front quarter at a point near the middle finger, Figure 72-A, and rolls or pivots the quarter upward against the thumb, Figure 72-B. Once the quarter has moved upward, it is an easy matter to tip the front quarter over the other quarter.

26.   REFLEXES

Hold a dollar bill at about the center between your right thumb and first finger. Place the left hand in a similar position on the other side of the bill, but keep the left fingers open. The position is shown in Figure 73.

Release the bill from the right hand and immediately catch it with the left, Figure 74. Repeat this a few times. It looks easy to catch the bill.

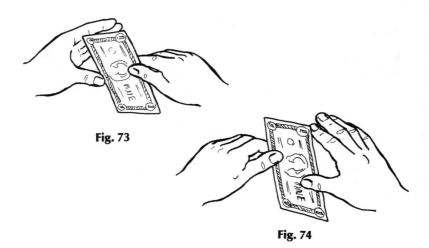

Fig. 73

Fig. 74

Ask the spectator if he would like to try it. Hold the bill at the midpoint between the right thumb and first finger. Have the spectator place his open left hand in the position shown in Figure 73.

Release the bill. It will slide past the spectator's hand before he is able to catch it. No matter how often the effect is repeated, the spectator will find it impossible to catch the bill.

27. METAL BENDING

Hold a half-dollar or a silver dollar at opposite edges of the coin between the tips of the thumbs and forefingers.

Rock the coin back and forth between the hands as shown in Figures 75 and 76. If you do this in front of a mirror you will see that a curious illusion is produced: the coin appears to bend as if made of rubber.

If you find a bent coin, keep it until ready to perform this stunt. The bent coin is kept in the pocket along with an unprepared coin. The unprepared coin is removed and the metal-bending illusion produced as described above.

The coin is dropped in the pocket. If the spectator appears skeptical, reach into the pocket and remove the bent coin. Enact the illusion again, then toss the bent coin out onto the table.

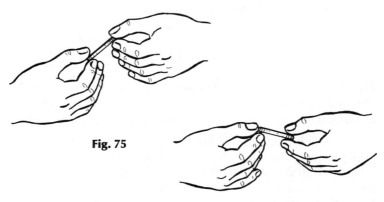

Fig. 75

Fig. 76

28. TOWER OF NICKELS

Ten nickels are stacked on top of one another. A dime is placed on top of the stack. The problem is to shift the position of the dime so it is second from the top of the stack of ten nickels. This is to be done without touching the stack, and it is to be accomplished in the shortest possible time.

Method: When the spectator gives up, remove another nickel from your pocket. In a quick motion flick it toward the stack, Figure 77, so it knocks the bottom coin out of the stack. Place this nickel on top of the stack and the problem is solved.

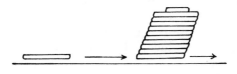

Fig. 77

The spectator may object, saying he thought you were not allowed to touch the coins, but that was not one of the conditions. All you said was that he was not allowed to touch the stack itself, not a coin propelled away from the stack.

The stack may be tilted or canted away from the direction of the incoming nickel. This increases the chances of the stack remaining intact when the bottom nickel is knocked out of the way.

29. BILLFLIP

Preliminary to some trick, the magician removes his billfold and places it at the near edge of the table. When he reaches for the billfold, it jumps into the air. The magician catches it in midflight.

Method: This stunt can be used with any trick in which you use paper money. For example, if performing "Bunco Bills" (No. 70), take the billfold from the pocket, remove the dollar bills, then place the billfold at the edge of the table as shown in Figure 78. The billfold should overhang the table's edge as much as possible without falling.

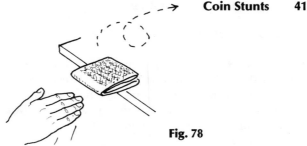

Fig. 78

Place the dollar bills on the table. Place both hands in the lap. Remark that you would like to demonstrate a trick using the bills. Notice the billfold. Say, "We won't need this."

The right hand comes up from the lap. The back of the hand hits the billfold, propelling it into the air. The billfold will turn over as shown by the arrow in Figure 78. The right hand, still palm down, catches the billfold while it is in the air.

When practicing, at first do not try to catch the billfold. Instead, concentrate on causing the billfold to flip as high as possible in the air. The stunt can also be done with a cased deck of playing cards. Only the brave will try it with a loose deck of cards.

30. SPREAD THE WEALTH

The magician draws the map shown in Figure 79. He explains that the straight lines represent roads. The points are labeled with the names of states. The magician mentions that Congress has come up with a new idea for the distribution of wealth.

The system is demonstrated by placing a coin on any state on the map, and then sliding the coin straight across a road to another

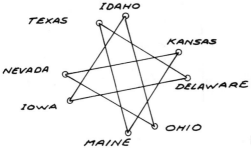

Fig. 79

state. For example, if a coin is placed on Nevada, it can be moved straight across to Kansas or Ohio.

Each time, a coin must be placed on a state that has no coin. The coin is then slid along a straight road to a state that does not have a coin. As the map gets filled up, it becomes harder to transfer money from state to state. The object is to use the above process to get a coin to seven of the eight states.

Method: The secret is simple but well concealed. Place a coin on Maine, then slide it to Kansas. Place the next coin on a state from which you can slide it to Maine. In the above example, place a coin on Texas and slide it to Maine.

The next coin is placed so that you can slide it to Texas. In the above example, place a coin on Delaware and slide it to Texas.

The pattern should be clear. Start by placing a coin on state *A* and sliding it to state *B*. Then place a coin on state *C* so that it can slide to state *A*. Place the next coin on state *D* so you can slide it to *C*, and so on.

In a sample solution, the sequence would be Maine to Kansas, Texas to Maine, Delaware to Texas, Iowa to Delaware, Idaho to Iowa, Ohio to Idaho, Nevada to Ohio. This clever presentation was suggested by Tom Fitzgerald.

31. PENNY HEX

This stunt is easy to do, but nearly impossible to reconstruct, even after the secret is demonstrated.

The problem is to start with six pennies arranged as in Figure 80, and transform the layout to the one shown in Figure 81 in the fewest number of moves. A move consists of sliding a coin to a new position so that it touches two other coins.

Fig. 80   **Fig. 81**   **Fig. 82**

It can be solved in three moves. Move 6 so it touches 4 and 5. Move 5 so it touches 2 and 3 from below. Move 3 so it touches 5 and 6.

Ask the spectator if he would like to try it. Pretend to arrange the coins in the position of Figure 80, but really arrange them as shown in Figure 82. If the spectator tries to mimic your moves, he will be unable to solve the puzzle.

32.   DATES

Where does the date 1776 appear on a dollar bill? Few will find it unless they know where to look. It is in the Roman numerals at the base of the pyramid.

33.   SNOW

Where is the anagram of "a night snow" on the dollar bill? "A night snow" is an anagram of Washington.

34.   KEY AND SCALE

Where is the key on a $1 bill? The scale? Both can be found in the seal, Figure 83.

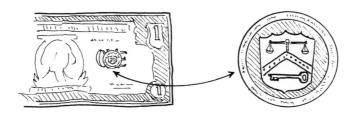

Fig. 83

35.   ON THE LINE

Draw a line on a piece of paper. The problem is to place three pennies on the paper so that there will be two heads on one side of the line and two tails on the other.

The solution is shown in Figure 84. If you have trouble keeping the coin upright, hold it in place with the hand.

Fig. 84

36.   TRIANGLE SOLITAIRE

Arrange ten coins on a piece of paper as shown in the layout of Figure 85. Draw a circle around each coin to mark its position. Then remove and discard one coin. This creates a vacant space on the layout.

Coins are now eliminated by the method of jumping used in checkers, i.e., one coin jumps over another and lands in the vacant space. The jumped-over coin is removed from play. The goal is to continue in this way until one coin remains on the layout.

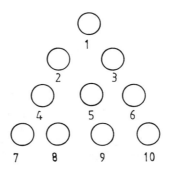

Fig. 85

As in checkers, a jump over one coin, then another, then another is considered a single move. What is the least number of moves required to win on the ten-coin layout?

It can be done in five moves by removing the coin at position 3, then jumping as follows. Jump 10 to 3, 1 to 6, 8 to 10 to 3, 4 to 6 to 1 to 4, 7 to 2.

37.   TOUCH FOUR

Can six pennies be arranged so each penny touches four others? The solution is to place four pennies on the table as in Figure 86. Then place the remaining two pennies as shown in Figure 87. You may have to hold them in place to keep them propped up.

Fig. 86

Fig. 87

38.   TWO-HEADED COIN

How many heads are there on a quarter? Two—Washington's head on one side and the head of the eagle on the other. This is sometimes expressed as a wager. Bet that you can change the spectator's quarter into a two-headed coin. Take the quarter, wave the hand over it, then show the head on each side. (The 1976 Bicentennial quarter has more than two heads.)

39.   HOW MANY EYES?

How many eyes are on a dollar bill? This is a double-catch question. Most people answer two for the two eyes on Washington. Then they remember there is an eye on top of the pyramid on the reverse side of the bill. But there is a *fourth* eye—the one on the eagle.

40.   BETTING LINCOLN

If a $5 bill is tossed in the air, what is the probability it will land with Lincoln's picture on top?

Lincoln's picture appears on the face of the bill. It is also in the Lincoln Memorial on the back of a $5 bill so, no matter how the bill lands, Lincoln's picture will be uppermost.

41.   NOT A HALF

The magician holds up his closed hand. He says, "I have two coins in my hand. They total 55 cents, but one of the coins is not a half-dollar. What are the two coins?"

The answer is that one coin is a nickel and the other is a half-dollar. When the magician opens his hand he points to the nickel and says, "That's the coin that's not the half-dollar."

42.   PENNY CATCH

Bet that you found a penny that has a head on one side and one on the other.

There is a head on one side and a "one" on the other.

43.   PENNY CHECKERS

Place eight pennies in a row as shown in Figure 88. Explain that a move consists of picking up a penny, jumping over two other pennies and placing the penny in hand on a single penny. In this way you are to form four stacked pairs of pennies. Can it be done in four moves?

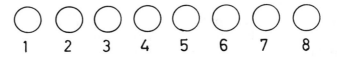

Fig. 88

The solution is to move 4 to 7, 6 to 2, 1 to 3, and 5 to 8. If you want to extend the puzzle so you start with ten pennies and have to end with five pairs, there is a simple solution. Jump 7 to 10. You now have a row of eight pennies and can proceed as already described.

44. HOW MANY ONES?

How many ones can be found on every dollar bill? The word "One" appears in eight places on all $1 bills. The numeral "1" appears in ten places. The reader should find eight 1's easily, but the other two are not immediately apparent. There is a 1 in the year of the series and a 1 in the date at the base of the pyramid.

45. DATE BET

Have the spectator put his hand into his change pocket and remove a coin in his closed fist. Ask him to guess the year on the coin. Bet him that you can guess a closer year if given two chances.

Whatever year he names, name the year before and the year after. For example, he names 1985. You would then name 1984 and 1986. Unless he hits the year exactly, one of your years must be closer to the year on the coin.

46. BALANCING ACT

Ask someone if he can balance a coin on the edge of a dollar bill. The spectator will give up after a few tries. You then take the coin and bill from him to show how it is done.

Fold the bill in half lengthwise. Then fold it in half widthwise. Make sure the folds are sharp.

Place the bill on the table and balance the coin on it as shown in Figure 89. Grasp the ends of the bill and pull the bill out straight

Fig. 89

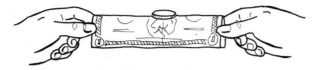

Fig. 90

with a smooth, steady action. The result will be that the coin rests on the edge of the bill as shown in Figure 90.

Try it with different-sized coins to see which works best. R. L. Cooper suggests that when the bill is in the straightened position shown in Figure 90 you can lift the bill off the table with the coin in the balanced position.

Another way to perform "Balancing Act" is to hand the spectator two dimes and the dollar bill. Ask if he thinks he can balance both coins on the edge of the bill at the same time. It seems an impossible feat. When he gives up, stack the two coins squarely on top of one another, then rest them on top of the bill, as shown in Figure 89. Proceed from there with the handling as written.

47. CONFUCIUS COINS

Ten dimes and ten pennies are placed in four rows of five coins each so dimes and pennies alternate, as shown in Figure 91. The problem is this: Using the first and second fingers of one hand, in one continuous move of any coins that can be touched, convert the layout to the one shown in Figure 92, where there is a row of pennies, a row of dimes, and so on. There can be no empty spaces. No row can be lengthened or shortened.

You will appreciate the solution much more if you try solving the problem before reading further.

Method: Emil Jarrow originated "Confucius Coins." In Figure 91, the two dimes in the top row are labeled *A* and *B*. Place the first finger on *A* and the second finger on *B*, Figure 93. Slide these two dimes up and out of the row. Then slide them around to the bottom of the layout.

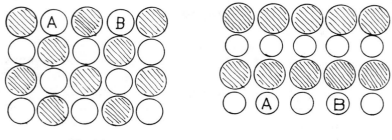

Fig. 91   Fig. 92

Fig. 93

Push *A* against the penny in the second position in the bottom row. Push *B* against the penny in the fourth position in the bottom row. As you push these coins upward, the two vertical rows will move upward.

The dimes labeled *A* and *B* will then take their places in the bottom row as shown in Figure 92.

The feat can be presented as a magical effect. Show the layout of Figure 91. Point out that the coins alternate in all rows and columns.

One hand then places a large square of cardboard over the layout to cover it. At the same time, the other hand performs the manipulation described above.

Once the layout has been covered and the move performed, snap the fingers, lift the cardboard to show that the layout has changed to the one shown in Figure 92. The distinct change in the layout is startling.

48.   SHARPER'S GAME

Twelve dimes and 12 pennies are arranged in the square layout shown in Figure 94. The spectator and the magician take turns making a move. A move consists in sliding a coin into the vacant space. The spectator gets silver, the magician copper.

A player loses when he is unable to make a move with one of his coins. If the spectator goes first, he must lose. This clever game was invented by G. W. Lewthwaite.

Method: The system is simple and requires no mental calculation. In Figure 95, the two coins marked with the letter A have the same date. Similarly, the two coins marked with the letter B have the same date. The dates on A-A are different from the dates on B-B.

In this way each pair of coins is identified by the fact that each coin of the pair has the same date. Thus the two coins at A-A might have the date 1980, the two coins at B-B might have 1975, the two coins at C-C might have 1990, and so forth.

When the spectator moves a silver coin into the vacant space, you follow by moving the copper coin of the same date into the new vacant space. Sooner or later the spectator will find it impossible to move.

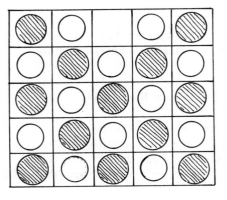

Fig. 94   Fig. 95

AT THE TABLE

After dinner, people are in a relaxed frame of mind, an ideal time for the performance of a few tricks with coins. The tricks in this chapter are particularly suited to being performed in the atmosphere that exists after the dessert dishes have been cleared away and people are in the mood to be entertained.

49. NIMBLE NICKELS

Ten nickels are placed on the table in two rows. Five of the coins are gathered in one hand, five in the other. One nickel is visibly transferred from the right hand to the left hand. Instantly, all ten nickels end up in the left hand.

This amazing trick was devised by David Devant and Dai Vernon.

Method: Any even number of similar coins can be used. If foreign coins are available, they will lend an exotic air to the trick.

For this discussion we will assume ten nickels are used. Arrange them on the table in two vertical rows, five coins in each row. The rows should be 6″–8″ apart.

Tell the audience that, with the new math, people may have forgotten how easy counting was in the old days. Grasp the two coins nearest you, one in each hand, between thumb and first finger. Turn the hands palm up. Close the fingers, but allow the coins to rest on the fingers, Figure 96. Say, "One and one."

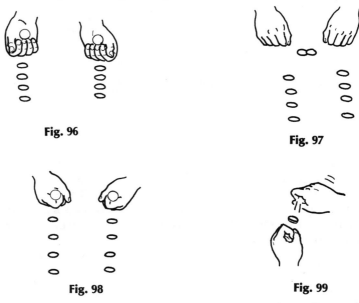

Fig. 96

Fig. 97

Fig. 98

Fig. 99

In a quick motion bring the hands together and simultaneously turn them palm down. Let the coins fall to the table, Figure 97. Say, "One and one is two."

Pick up the coins, one in each hand, keeping the fingers closed into fists. Let the coins rest momentarily on top of the fists, Figure 98. Then open the fists slightly, allowing the coins to fall into the fists.

Grasp the next pair of coins in the hands as shown in Figure 96. Turn the hands palm down in a quick motion as before, with the hands being momentarily brought together. But this time open the left fingers just enough to catch secretly the coin that rests on the fingers. At the same time, open the right fingers enough to allow the coin in the right fist to fall to the table.

The result is as shown in Figure 97. The audience sees two coins fall to the table. The spectators are unaware both coins came from the right hand.

Pick up these two coins on top of the fists, Figure 98. Allow the coins to sink into the clenched fists. The audience thinks each hand holds two coins. Actually, the left hand holds three coins, the right hand just one. As the above sequence is performed, say, "And two more coins make four."

Perform exactly the same actions with the third, fourth and fifth pairs of coins. As you do, say, "Two more make six." "Two more make eight." "Two more make ten." At this point, with all coins gathered in the fists, you will have nine coins in the left hand and one in the right.

Say, "Of course when you get to ten, you have to remember to carry the one." As you say this, tip the right fist over onto the left, so the single coin in the right fist can be dropped onto the left fist, Figure 99. Allow the coin to slip into the closed left hand.

Say, "Ten is made from a zero and a one. We have zero over here." Open the right hand to show it empty. "And ten over here." Open the left hand, allowing the ten coins to pour out onto the table.

50. TWIST

A coin is wrapped in a handkerchief. The spectator pulls the ends of the handkerchief. The coin vanishes. The handkerchief is waved over a saltshaker. The spectator lifts the saltshaker and finds the missing coin under it.

Method: Required are an opaque handkerchief, a quarter and a duplicate quarter. Beforehand, secretly place the quarter under a saltshaker or other object on the table.

Spread the handkerchief out flat on the table. Place the other quarter in the center, Figure 100.

Fold the bottom half up, Figure 101. Fold the right half over to

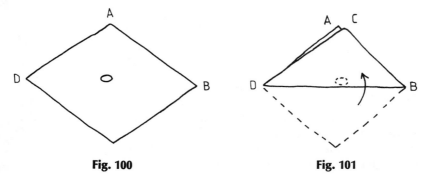

Fig. 100   **Fig. 101**

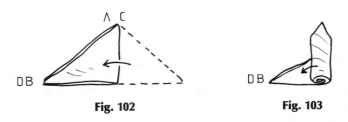

Fig. 102   **Fig. 103**

the left, Figure 102. Roll the handkerchief from right to left, Figure 103, until ends *B* and *D* flip under and around to the top. The spectator grasps the ends as shown in Figure 104.

Explain and pantomime with the hands that he is to lift the handkerchief off the table and pull the ends sharply apart. When this is done by the spectator it will appear that the coin has vanished. Actually, the coin is trapped inside the center of the handkerchief, as shown in Figure 105.

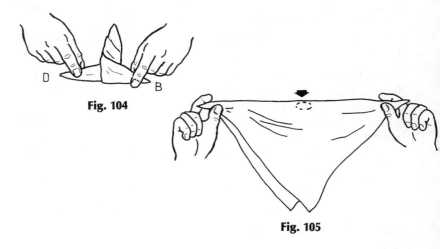

Fig. 104

Fig. 105

Grasp the coin through the cloth at the point marked by the arrow shown in Figure 105. Taking the handkerchief from the spectator, wave it over the saltshaker.

Let the spectator lift the saltshaker to reveal the coin. Place the handkerchief, with the concealed coin, in the pocket.

51. PENNY ANTE

Two pennies placed on the table are covered with the hands. On command, both pennies end up under the same hand.

Method: To perform this trick, the palms of the hands should be moist. Place two pennies on the table about 12″ apart. Cover the coins with the hands, Figure 106.

Lift the hands and cross them, left over right, Figure 107. Shake your head as if conditions are not quite right. Draw the hands away and make some minor adjustment to the coins.

Cover the coins as in Figure 106. Then cross the hands, left over right, and cover the coins as in Figure 107.

Press firmly on the coin under the right hand so the coin adheres to the palm. Begin to uncross the hands but let the left hand move faster than the right so the left hand is over the right just as the right hand lifts away from the table, Figure 108. This conceals the fact that the coin on the left is being stolen under the right hand.

Bring the hands back to the position shown in Figure 106. Lift the left hand to reveal that its coin has vanished. Then lift the right hand to show both coins.

As a variation, you can have a dime and penny on the left, a dime on the right. Perform the above trick, but steal the dime on the left, leaving the penny. The result is that both dimes end up on the right.

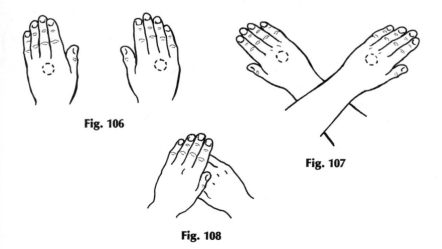

Fig. 106

Fig. 107

Fig. 108

52. MOBILITY

Three coins are placed in a triangular layout as shown in Figure 109. Two of the coins are covered with playing cards. One coin vanishes from under its card and appears under the other card.

Method: The routine is based on an idea of Jacob Daley's. Place three quarters in the layout shown in Figure 109. The trick should be done on a table covered with a tablecloth.

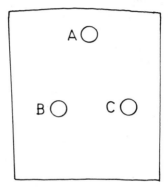

Fig. 109

Take a playing card in each hand. Cover the coin at *A* with the card in the left hand. At the same time cover the coin at *C* with the card in the right hand.

Shake your head. Say, "No, I don't feel a psychic connection between these two coins."

Cover the coin at *B* with the card in the left hand. At the same time, cover the coin at *C* with the card in the right hand. Again shake your head and say, "Still no connection."

The right-hand card is now placed at position *B*. The left hand moves its card forward to position *A*. But as it does so, the back of the left hand contacts the coin at *B* and secretly slides it up to position *A*. An exposed view of the sliding action is shown in Figure 110.

The hands are now in the position shown in Figure 111. Release the cards. Say, "Here's the psychic connection I was looking for." Pick up the coin at position *C*. Openly place it under the card at position *A*.

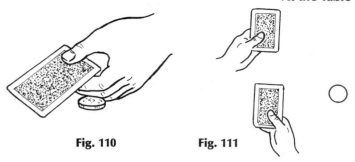

Fig. 110   **Fig. 111**

Snap the fingers. Pick up the card at *B* to show that the coin has vanished. Pick up the card at position *A* to reveal all three coins.

If asked to repeat this trick, follow up with "Two Coins" (No. 61) or "Astral Coins" (No. 68).

53.   DOWN UNDER

"There are several magicians living in this building," the magician says. "Sometimes we'll do a trick together. I'll throw a coin invisibly to the fellow upstairs. His friend downstairs will toss it back."

So saying, the magician wraps a coin in a handkerchief. He tosses it toward the ceiling. The coin vanishes. The magician downstairs gets the coin on the relay and tosses it back. The coin is heard to rattle around on the floor at the spectator's feet.

Method: Two identical coins are used. While seated at the table, secretly place one coin on the edge of the knee. Raise the heel so your foot rests on the toe. This prevents the coin from sliding off the knee, Figure 112.

Fig. 112

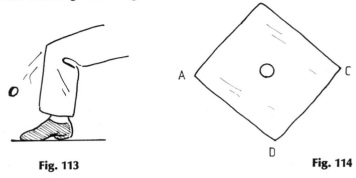

Fig. 113   **Fig. 114**

Later, when you want the coin to fall to the floor, lower the heel to the floor, Figure 113. The coin will fall off the knee and clatter to the floor.

With a coin on the knee as shown in Figure 112, spread an opaque handkerchief out flat on the table. Place a coin in the center of the handkerchief, Figure 114. Fold the bottom half up to the top, Figure 115.

Grasp corner A between the left thumb and first finger. At the same time, grasp corners B and D with the right hand and transfer these two corners to a position between the left first and second fingers.

Finally, grasp corner C with the right hand and bring it under the left thumb. The situation is shown in Figure 116.

Shake the handkerchief bag gently as you tell about your magician friends living above and below. Then grasp corner C between the right thumb and first finger. Release corners B and D.

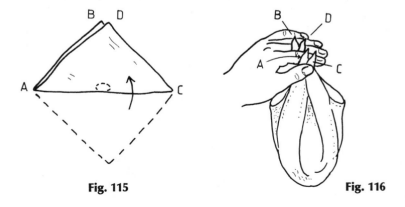

Fig. 115   **Fig. 116**

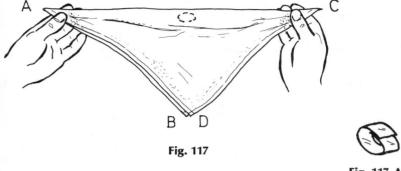

Fig. 117

Fig. 117-A

At the same time, with a sharp motion, extend the hands so the handkerchief is pulled taut, Figure 117. Raise the hands upward as they are pulled apart, and look toward the ceiling as if following the flight of the coin. Actually, the coin is trapped in a fold of the handkerchief.

Drop your gaze to the floor. At the same time lower the heel to the floor, Figure 113. The coin on the knee will clatter to the floor, apparently having completed its invisible round-trip. As the spectators look for the coin that has just rolled to the floor, lower the handkerchief to the table. Fold it up and place it in the pocket to get rid of the duplicate coin.

If you find that the coin does not remain concealed inside the handkerchief in Figure 117, there is a surefire alternate method. Roll a small piece of transparent tape into a cylinder with the sticky or adhesive side outward, Figure 117-A. Place this piece of tape in the center of the handkerchief. This completes the preparation.

When performing the trick, spread the handkerchief out on the table with the tape side up. Place a coin on the center of the handkerchief as shown in Figure 114. The coin is placed directly onto the tape.

Proceed with the trick as written. When you reach the point illustrated in Figure 117, the coin will remain hidden inside the handkerchief because it adheres to the tape.

Home-improvement stores sell transparent tape that has adhesive on both sides. Carpet tape also has adhesive on both sides. If you find that the tape shows up on a white handkerchief, use a handkerchief with an allover pattern to conceal the tape.

54. COVER UP

Yank Ho invented a coin trick in which coins placed in a square layout magically gather together. The following is a simplified handling of this classic plot.

Method: Required are two playing cards and four similar coins. Assume the coins are half-dollars. Place the coins in a layout measuring 8″ square. Each hand holds a playing card between the first and second finger. The starting position is shown in Figure 118.

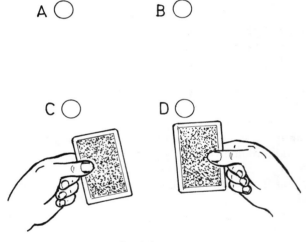

Fig. 118

Remark that coins sometimes act in sympathy with one another. As you speak, cover the coin at A with the left-hand card, the coin at D with the right-hand card.

Then cover the coin at C with the left-hand card; the coin at B with the right-hand card.

The secret maneuver comes into play here. Cover the coin at A with the left-hand card, the coin at C with the right-hand card. Make sure the right first finger, under the card, rests at the right edge of the coin at C.

Slide the left-hand card to a position under the coin at C, Figure

119. This will raise the coin off the table, allowing the coin to be clipped secretly by the right first finger. The right first finger presses the coin against the card held by the right hand. This maneuver was devised by James Drilling.

The left hand leaves its card at C. The right hand places its card at position A, Figure 120. When placing the right-hand card on the table, be sure the hidden coin does not clink against the coin already at A.

Say, "You've heard the expression that birds of a feather flock together. Here's what that means." Take the coin at B in the right hand. Place the right hand under the table.

Clink the right hand's coin against the underside of the table. Lift the card at A to show two coins. One coin apparently penetrated up through the table to join the coin at A.

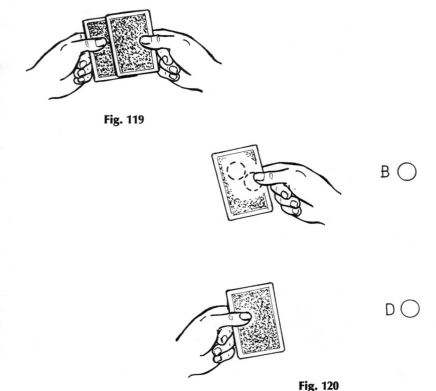

Fig. 119

B ◯

D ◯

Fig. 120

Pick up the two coins at *A* with the left hand. Bring the palm-up right hand to a position just below the near edge of the tabletop. Drop the two coins from the left hand into the right hand.

Bring the right hand into view. It is cupped so the audience cannot get a clear view of the coins. Drop all three coins from the right hand to the left hand.

Place the left hand palm down at *B*. The right hand takes the coin at *D* and places it under the table.

The right hand taps its coin against the underside of the tabletop. At the same time, the left hand opens so its three coins drop into view. Apparently another coin has penetrated the table.

The palm-up right hand moves to a position just below the edge of the tabletop. The left hand drops its three coins into the right hand.

Close the right hand into a fist. Place it palm down at *D*. Tap the card at *C* with the left hand. Turn up this card to show that the last coin has vanished.

Open the right hand to reveal all four coins.

In working the routine, if you find you have trouble keeping two coins concealed under the card at the position shown in Figure 120, you can use cardboard squares measuring 3″ on a side or larger.

55.   DUET

Coins of different denominations are wrapped in a handkerchief. The spectator is asked to name one. The named coin penetrates the tabletop, leaving the other coin wrapped in the handkerchief.

Method: This routine is based on a means of secretly transferring a coin from inside the handkerchief to the lap. John V. Hope and Robert Olsen devised a brilliant method that requires no sleight of hand.

You may wish to drape a napkin over the lap to keep the coin from falling to the floor. Also, it may be necessary to sit so that the toes touch the floor but the heels are raised. This tends to raise the knees and will keep the coin from falling or rolling off.

Spread a handkerchief out flat on the table so one corner is over the near edge of the table. Place a nickel and a half-dollar on the center of the handkerchief. The half-dollar is toward you. The position is shown in Figure 121.

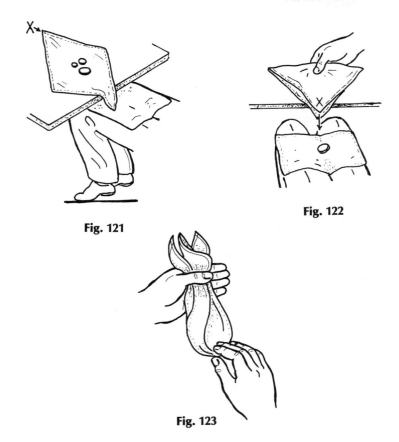

Fig. 121

Fig. 122

Fig. 123

The far corner, marked X in Figure 121, is brought down and over the coins so this corner is just at the near edge of the table. The right hand grasps the nickel through the handkerchief.

As the handkerchief is raised off the table, the half-dollar will slide out and into the lap as shown in Figure 122. The folds of the handkerchief cover the movement of the coin. Make sure the near edge of the handkerchief is not lifted from the table until the coin slides into the lap.

Turn the left hand palm up and grasp the handkerchief just above the coins as shown in Figure 123. Show the right hand empty. Place it below the table. When it is out of sight, the right hand grasps the half-dollar and brings it to a position under the table.

Ask the spectator, "Which coin would you like to have?" Nine times out of ten, he will name the half-dollar. Bring the handkerchief down so the center touches the table. At the same time, rap the half-dollar against the underside of the table. Then bring the half-dollar into view and toss it onto the table. Allow the spectator to open the handkerchief to reveal the other coin.

Should the spectator name the nickel, reply, "Then that leaves the half-dollar for me." Cause the half-dollar to penetrate the tabletop as described above. Hand the handkerchief to the spectator and have him discover that the nickel remains inside.

SWINDLE SWITCH

In *Modern Magic,* Professor Hoffmann describes a move of Robert Houdin's that has many uses. Some applications of this versatile idea will be described in this chapter.

56. THE MASKED MOVE

A coin and a dollar bill are covered with a handkerchief. The spectator names either piece of money. If he chooses the coin, it immediately penetrates the handkerchief, leaving the bill inside.

Method: Hold a half-dollar between the left thumb and first finger. Cover the coin with a handkerchief. Grasp the coin through the fabric of the handkerchief with the right thumb and first finger, Figure 124.

Fig. 124

The left thumb now adjusts its grip. It folds an additional layer of cloth against the coin. This is shown in the view of Figure 125. The right hand can aid in this action.

The right hand now grips the front hem of the handkerchief, Figure 126. It brings this portion of the handkerchief back to the left arm, Figure 127. This is done to remind the spectator that the coin is under the handkerchief.

In Figure 126, the rear hem of the handkerchief is indicated by an X. When the front hem is brought back to the position shown in Figure 127, the right thumb slips under the rear hem at the position marked X.

The right hand grasps both hems at this point and brings them

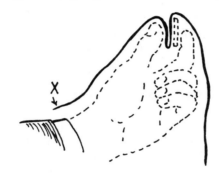

Fig. 125

Fig. 126

Fig. 127

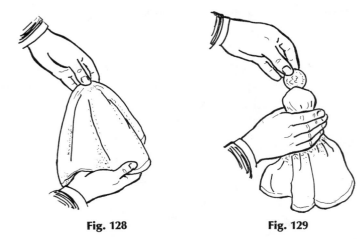

Fig. 128   Fig. 129

down and over the coin to the position shown in Figure 128. It appears that the coin is still under the handkerchief, but now the coin is in back of the handkerchief.

Display a dollar bill that has been folded in eighths. Place it under the handkerchief. Hold it in place through the cloth with the left thumb. It appears as if the bill and the coin are now under the handkerchief. Give the spectator a choice of either piece of money.

Regardless of how the spectator responds, curl the right fingers around the handkerchief at a point just below the coin. The left thumb and first finger slowly pull the coin upward, Figure 129. The illusion is that the coin penetrated the handkerchief.

If the spectator names the coin, say, "Here it is," as you produce the coin. If he names the bill, say, "That leaves the coin for me," as you produce the coin and place it in your pocket.

In either case, once the coin has been produced, unfold the handkerchief to show the bill still in the center. This clever use of the Swindle Switch was developed by Jean Hugard.

57. THRU THE RING

Stewart Judah featured a trick in which a borrowed coin apparently passed through a borrowed finger ring. The ring was much smaller than the coin, yet the coin passed through the ring without harming it.

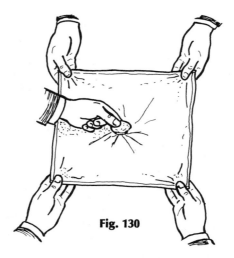

Fig. 130

Method: The coin is wrapped in the handkerchief as illustrated in Figures 124–128. Hold the coin in place while a spectator gathers the ends of the handkerchief and slips them through the borrowed ring.

Have two spectators grasp the corners of the handkerchief. The situation at this point is shown in Figure 130. You still grasp the coin through the thickness of the cloth with the left hand. It appears as if the coin has been trapped by the ring.

Have the spectator pull the corners of the handkerchief to increase tension of the fabric. Then grasp the ring with the right hand.

Both hands move upward. The right hand has the ring, while the left comes away with the coin. It is a striking effect.

58. LOCKPICK

Covering a coin with a handkerchief, the magician says, "Once I met a fellow who could pick locks. I don't have a bank vault handy, but pretend that, when this coin is under the handkerchief, it's been locked in a safe."

The magician then places a key on the outside of the handkerchief. He says, "Remember the money is in the vault." Snapping his

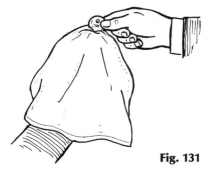

Fig. 131

fingers, he causes the coin to change places with the key. The coin is outside the handkerchief and the key inside.

Method: This transposition effect was devised by the author. Display a coin between the left thumb and first finger. Cover it with a handkerchief, Figure 124. Then display a key. Place it on the outside of the handkerchief against the coin. The key is shown in Figure 131. It is held in place against the coin with the left thumb.

Lift the front hem of the handkerchief to display the coin once more as you say, "Remember, the coin is locked in the safe." Grasp both the front and the back hem, Figure 127, and bring them down in front to the position shown in Figure 128.

Snap the fingers. Then grasp the handkerchief with the right hand at the point indicated in Figure 129. Extract the coin with the left thumb and first finger as you say, "Now the coin is on the outside."

Place the coin aside. Lift the front hem of the handkerchief to display the key as you add, "And the key is inside."

59.   MILLER'S MAGIC

This one-hand method of causing a borrowed coin to penetrate a handkerchief was invented by Jack Miller.

Grasp the coin between the left thumb and first finger. As the right hand covers the coin with the handkerchief, the left hand

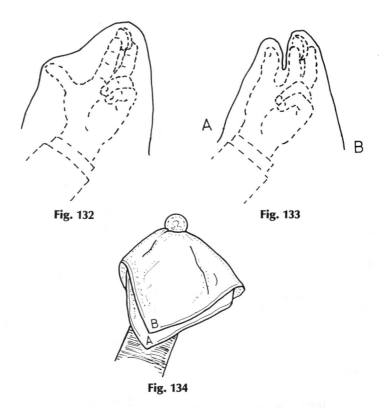

Fig. 132

Fig. 133

Fig. 134

shifts its grip so the coin is grasped between the first and second fingers, Figure 132.

The left thumb is extended back toward the body as shown in Figure 132. Then the thumb moves forward, trapping a fold of cloth against the coin, Figure 133. If the skin is dry, the thumb may slide along without catching the cloth. In this event, when the left hand is in the position of Figure 132, push down on the cloth between the thumb and the coin with the right fingers. This creates a depression in the cloth that allows you to clip the cloth against the coin as shown in Figure 133.

Flip end B up over the arm to display the coin, Figure 134. Note that in Figure 134 only the coin shows.

Now flip ends A and B down and over the coin to bring you to the position shown in Figure 135. The audience thinks the coin is under the handkerchief.

Fig. 135

Fig. 136

Grip the coin between the left thumb and first finger. Curl the left second, third and fourth fingers around the handkerchief at a point under the cloth, Figure 136. Then curl the left first finger around the handkerchief.

Slowly work the coin out of the handkerchief with the left fingers. It will appear that the coin has magically penetrated the center of the handkerchief.

PREPARED TRICKS

Coins and bills are used in money transactions of everyday life. Because they are common objects, they are not suspected of being prepared or gimmicked. This is an advantage for the magician because he can perform strong magic with the aid of prepared coins or bills.

When putting together a routine of several money tricks, it is acceptable to include one or two prepared tricks of the kind described in this chapter. If too many such tricks are performed at the same time, the audience cannot help but note that the apparatus is acting with exceptional strangeness, and they will conclude that unseen aids are at work. But when properly chosen and strategically placed, prepared tricks can elevate a magic act to the miracle class.

60. HALF AND HALF

Ideas of Jimmy Herpick and Louis Tannen are combined to produce this novel trick. A borrowed dollar bill is placed in an envelope. The spectator initials the flap of the envelope to avoid the suspicion of a switch. While the magician holds the ends of the envelope, the spectator cuts the envelope in half. The bill has now been cut in halves. When the performer shakes out the two halves of the bill, they have changed to half-dollars.

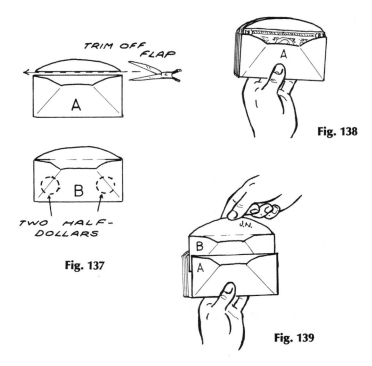

Fig. 138

Fig. 137

Fig. 139

Method: Two envelopes are prepared beforehand. Trim off the flap from one envelope (envelope *A* in Figure 137). Place two half-dollars into another envelope (envelope *B* in Figure 137). One half-dollar is on each side of the envelope.

Place envelope *A* on top of envelope *B*. Then place these two prepared envelopes on top of four or five envelopes. This stack of envelopes can be carried in the pocket until you are ready to perform.

Borrow a dollar bill. Slide it into envelope *A* until all but about a half-inch of the bill is inside the envelope. The situation is shown in Figure 138. Have the spectator write his initials on the inside of the flap. Unknown to him, the uppermost flap is really that of envelope *B*. The protruding bill hides the fact that envelope *A* has no flap.

When the spectator has signed his initials on the flap, push the dollar bill all the way into envelope *A*. Grasp the flap of envelope *B* and pull this envelope upward, Figure 139.

Fig. 140

Place the other envelopes in the pocket. Seal the flap of envelope *B*. Hold the envelope as shown in Figure 140, so that each hand holds a coin in place.

Have the spectator cut the envelope in half, Figure 140. Remark that the bill has been cut in halves. Then allow the half-dollars to fall out onto the table.

61.   TWO COINS

Two coins, covered with playing cards, behave in increasingly strange ways. In one effect, each coin is covered with a playing card. With no moves, one coin vanishes and appears under the other card. In another effect, one coin mysteriously clings to the bottom of a playing card, then drops to join the other coin.

Method: Two nickels are joined by a piece of fine thread, Figure 141. The thread is taped to the bottom of each coin. The thread should be about 1½″ long.

Start with the nickels in the pocket along with some loose change. Remove a handful of change, pick out the prepared set of nickels and place them on the table. The taped sides of the coins are on the bottom and thus out of the spectator's view.

Cover one of the nickels with a playing card, Figure 142. As the

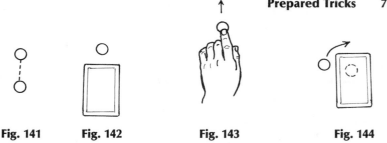

Fig. 141   **Fig. 142**   **Fig. 143**   **Fig. 144**

right hand picks up the other card, the left hand slides the visible nickel forward, Figure 143. Unknown to the audience, as the visible nickel is slid forward, the other nickel is secretly stolen out from under its card. The stolen nickel is hidden by the left wrist.

The right hand drops its playing card on top of the visible nickel, at the same time covering the other nickel as well. Snap your fingers, pick up the first card and show that the coin has vanished. Then pick up the other card to show both nickels.

For the repeat, place the nickels side by side as indicated in Figure 144. Cover the nickel on the right with a card. The left first finger pushes the visible coin up and around to a position in front of the card, Figure 144. This simple maneuver helps strengthen the illusion that the coins are not connected.

The right hand picks up the other card and, as indicated in Figure 145, uses the card to slide the visible coin forward. Again the other coin is secretly stolen; when you drop the card onto the visible coin, the card actually rests on top of *both* coins.

Snap your fingers over the first card, lift it and show that the coin has vanished. Then lift the other card to reveal both coins.

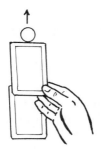

Fig. 145

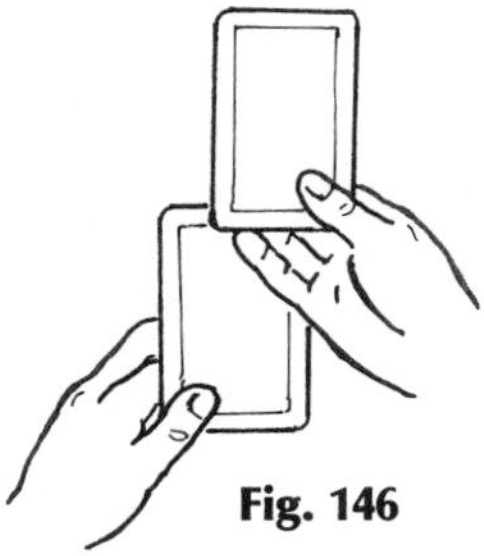

Fig. 146

Fig. 147

Fig. 148

The trick can be repeated one more time with a different handling. Place the two nickels on the table, Figure 141. Place a card over the lower nickel with the left hand. Grip the card between the thumb and first finger. Do not release your grip on the card.

With the right hand cover the visible nickel. As this is done, the left second finger drags its coin back under cover of the card still held by the left hand. The position of the hands when the steal is made is shown in Figure 146. The result is that both coins will lie under the lower card. With this move, note that the steal is made without visibly moving either coin.

The right hand continues its forward motion and drops its card on what is apparently the other coin. Snap the fingers. Then show that both nickels are under the lower card.

For the final trick, place the two nickels side by side. Cover the rightmost nickel with a card. Then slide the other nickel to the left, Figure 147. As before, the nickel under the right card is secretly stolen and is now under the card on the left.

With the left hand, place the leftmost coin on top of its playing card. The card has a coin under it and one over it at this point.

Wave the hand over the rightmost card. Gently lift this card off the table about two or three inches. Remark that the nickel will cling mysteriously to the bottom of this card. Bring this card over the other card, Figure 148. Lower it gently. When it touches the visible coin, pull the leftmost card away with a quick action. The two coins will clink against one another. Turn both cards over and toss them out onto the table. Scoop up the coins and return them to the pocket.

The above routine uses ideas of Mort Rudnick, Harvey Rosenthal, John Bowery and the author. If you find the thread has a tendency to show up on the table, perform the trick with a newspaper or magazine as a working surface.

62. POROUS COIN

A borrowed coin is wrapped in a piece of newspaper. A needle or hatpin is repeatedly pushed through the coin. At the finish the borrowed coin is returned undamaged to the spectator.

Method: This trick uses a coin fold invented by H. G. A. Lambie. Use a square of newspaper from the classified pages. It should measure 5½" square. Fold it in thirds each way and then unfold it.

A strip of newspaper 5½" long and 1⅞" wide is then glued to the bottom third of the large square. Glue is applied to the end sections shown shaded in Figure 149. The result is that a center pocket is formed through which the coin can slide. Turn the apparatus over side for side.

Fold the bottom third up onto the center. Then place a borrowed quarter into the secret pocket, Figure 150. Show the coin apparently being placed on the center square of the paper. It is a perfect illusion.

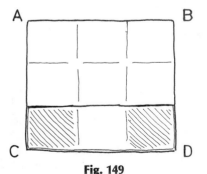

Fig. 149

Fig. 150

Fig. 151

Fold the top third down. Then fold the left third over to the right and the right third over to the left. The coin is apparently trapped inside the folded paper.

Grasp the folded newspaper with the left hand. The right hand removes a needle or hatpin from the lapel or from the pocket. The point of the needle is pushed against the center of the paper. At the same time, the left hand releases pressure, allowing the coin to slide down to the position shown in Figure 151.

This allows the needle to penetrate the center of the paper and, apparently, the center of the coin. Repeat this penetration a few more times. Then replace the hatpin in the pocket. Tear off the top of the newspaper and dump the coin out undamaged. Place the newspaper in the pocket.

63. MONEYFLY

A spectator removes a penny, nickel, dime and quarter from his pocket. The magician takes one coin and causes it to vanish. That coin reappears inside the spectator's closed fist.

Method: The routine is based on a clever idea of Ron Edwards. Cut the oval picture of George Washington from a play dollar bill and paste it onto the picture of Washington on another bill. The glued portion, shown shaded in Figure 152, runs halfway around the oval. When in place, this extra oval forms a pocket that is open at the right. To complete the preparation, drop a dime into the pocket. The dime is shown by the dotted lines in Figure 152.

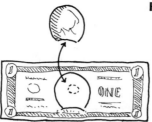

Fig. 152

Fig. 153 **Fig. 154**

Borrow a penny, nickel, dime and quarter from the spectator. Hold the prepared bill face up in the left palm. Drop the borrowed coins onto the bill. Pretend to study the coins. Then say you will use the dime. Place the dime on the table.

Have the spectator hold his right hand palm up. Slide the other coins off the bill onto his palm. As you do, the dime inside the pocket is secretly added to the other coins, Figure 153. Note that the bill blocks the coins from the spectator's view. Keep the bill in this position until the spectator closes his fist.

Have the spectator turn his fist palm down. This will keep him from opening his hand until the right moment.

Hold the prepared bill so the side with the pocket is toward you. Pick up the borrowed dime from the table between the right thumb and first finger.

Place the dime on the prepared side of the bill. Slide the right hand downward, Figure 154. At the same time, allow the dime to slide into the pocket. Keeping the bill in the upright position of Figure 154, wave it over your right hand, then over the spectator's right hand. Open your right hand to show that the dime is gone. Have the spectator turn his hand palm up. He then opens his hand to discover that the dime has apparently returned.

64.   SAFE DEPOSIT

Magicians can send money into safe-deposit boxes by means of teleportation. To show how the process works, the magician uses a $1 bill of his own and a borrowed $5 bill. They are folded and displayed as in Figure 155.

On command, the $5 bill vanishes and is found in a cardboard box on view from the start of the routine.

Method: Cut the "5" from the upper right corner on the back of a play $5 bill. Glue it to the upper right corner on the front of a $1 bill, Figure 156.

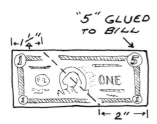

Fig. 155

Fig. 156

You are going to fold the prepared bill so it looks like two bills. Crease the bill along the dotted lines as shown in Figure 156. Then fold the left portion over onto the right portion. The bill now looks like Figure 157.

Crease the left side of the bill along the dotted lines shown in Figure 157. Then fold the shaded portion around in back. The bill will look like Figure 158.

Crease the bill along the dotted lines shown in Figure 158. Then fold the shaded portion in back. The result is the bill as shown in Figure 159.

This is how the bill is folded. Practice it a few times. Once the handling becomes familiar to you, unfold the bill, and place it in the pocket until the time of performance.

Show a cardboard box empty. Place it on the table. Remark that it will act the role of safe-deposit box. Ask for the loan of a $5 bill. As the spectator removes the $5 bill from his pocket, remove the prepared dollar bill from your pocket. Toss both bills into the box.

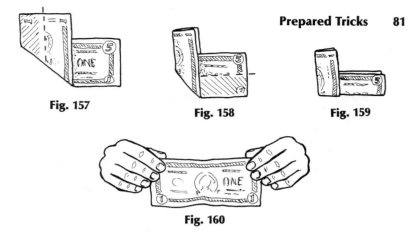

Fig. 157

Fig. 158

Fig. 159

Fig. 160

Explain that a magician can teleport money into a safe-deposit box. Reach into the box and fold the prepared bill as described above. Then pretend to fold the $5 bill in quarters, keeping the bill in the box and out of the spectator's sight.

Remove the folded $1 bill and display it as shown in Figure 155. It will look like two separate bills. Crumple the bill, then open it, Figure 160, so the hand covers the prepared corner. It will appear to the audience that the $5 bill has vanished. Let the spectator look in the box for the missing $5 bill.

65. MAGNETIZO

The magician removes two bills from his wallet. He rubs the bills on his jacket sleeve to create static electricity. Then he causes the bills to cling to one another in improbable ways, Figure 161.

Fig. 161

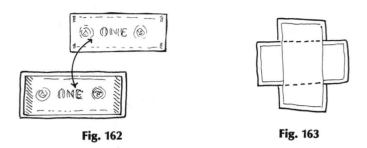

Fig. 162   **Fig. 163**

Method: Using rubber cement, coat the back of one play-money bill at each end in the shaded areas shown in Figure 162. Trim the border away from another bill, Figure 162. Fasten the borderless bill to the treated side of the other bill. Properly done, the preparation cannot be detected when the bill is shown front and back. The prepared bill can be carried in the wallet along with a matching unprepared play-money bill.

To perform, rub the prepared bill on the jacket sleeve. Place it, prepared side down, on the table. Rub the borrowed bill on the jacket sleeve.

Place the unprepared bill on top of the prepared bill. Lift the unprepared bill. The prepared bill remains on the table.

Rub the unprepared bill on the sleeve again as you remark you have not generated enough static electricity. Then slide this bill between the two pasted bills as shown in the exposed view of Figure 163. The right hand, grasping the prepared bill, can then lift both bills off the table as if they were clinging to one another.

Repeat the trick once or twice, aligning the bills at different angles. Then pocket the prepared bill. If the spectator wants to try it, remove an unprepared bill from the pocket and hand it over.

66.   MYSTIC DIME

Two half-dollars are dropped into a cup. The cup is placed on the table. Two other half-dollars and a mystic dime are dropped into another cup and this cup is placed under the table. One at a time, the two half-dollars from the first cup are heard to penetrate the table and drop into the other cup. No extra coins are used.

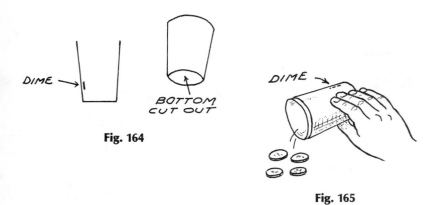

Fig. 164

Fig. 165

Method: Two opaque flat-bottomed paper drinking cups are used. They should measure at least 5″ in height. This ensures that the spectator cannot look down into the cups and spot the secret.

Cut the bottom from one cup. Slide a dime into the other cup so the dime rests against the side of the cup. This is shown in Figure 164.

Nest the bottomless cup in the other cup. The dime is now trapped between the two cups. Drop four half-dollars into the nested cups.

To present the routine, tip the nested cups over to allow the four half-dollars to fall out. As you do this, say, "There are four half-dollars in this cup." The dime is still trapped between the cups, Figure 165.

Straighten up the cups. Remove the bottomless cup and place it on the table. Then say, "And a mystic dime in this cup." Now tip the unprepared cup over and allow the dime to fall out. Because different coins seem to come from different cups, it appears as if the two cups are unprepared.

Nest the bottomless cup in the unprepared cup. Then arrange all coins heads up on the table. Say, "This dime was given to me by a magician who said it had mystic powers."

Pick up two half-dollars and drop them, one at a time, into the nested cups. Grip the nested cups from above with the palm-down left hand. Lift the two cups slightly off the table. Grip the unprepared cup near its base with the right hand.

The left hand removes the bottomless cup and places it down to

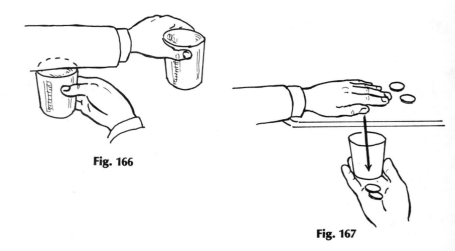

Fig. 166

Fig. 167

the right, Figure 166. At the same time, the right hand taps its cup against the table just hard enough to cause the coins inside to clink. Synchronize the sound so it is produced just as the bottomless cup touches the table. This produces the illusion that the sound comes from the coins that are supposed to be in the bottomless cup.

Place the right hand palm up in the lap. Place the unprepared cup in the right palm. The left hand then picks up the two half-dollars on the table and apparently drops them into this cup. The coins actually hit the side of the cup and fall into the right palm, Figure 167. Pick up the dime, saying, "The mystic dime casts the spell." Drop the dime into the cup.

Place the cup under the table. Pause, then say, "The dime isn't quite ready." Take the unprepared cup with the left hand and empty the contents onto the table. The audience sees two half-dollars and the dime, so all appears honest. The right hand remains under the table. Unknown to the audience, there are two half-dollars in the right hand.

Drop the two half-dollars and the dime into the unprepared cup.

The cup is placed in the lap, but really is held between the knees. The left hand is then placed palm down on top of the bottomless cup. Command the coins to leave this cup.

Drop one coin from the right hand into the cup that is on the lap. Pause a moment, then drop the other coin into the cup.

Shake the bottomless cup with the left hand to demonstrate it is empty. At the same time bring the other cup into view. Tip it over to allow the four half-dollars and the dime to fall to the table.

67. TOPSY-TURVY

The magician places three copper and three silver coins taken from a saucer full of coins into a change purse. An empty change purse is picked up and held in the other hand.

On command, the three copper coins leave the first purse and materialize in the second purse.

Method: Inexpensive imitation-leather change purses are available in department stores. Two are needed for this trick.

Open one of the purses. With a pair of scissors cut a slit in one side. The slit should be wide enough for a coin to fall through easily. Open the other purse. Place three copper pennies into this purse. Close the purse and turn it over. Shake this purse so the three pennies gather at the top near a corner. Place the purse in the pocket in this inverted condition.

A handful of dimes and pennies are placed on a saucer. This completes the preparation.

When presenting the trick, pick up the purse that has a slit in it. Hold the purse so the side with the slit is toward you and therefore concealed from audience view.

Display the saucer of coins. Place it on the table in front of you. The purse with the slit is rested on the saucer.

Pick up a dime, show it and drop it into the purse. Do the same with two more dimes. Then pick up a penny, display it and drop it into the purse, but feed it through the slit so it falls out of the purse and back into the saucer, Figure 168. Do the same thing with two

Fig. 168

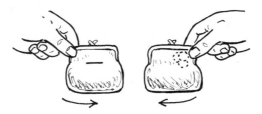

Fig. 169

more pennies. (If you find the sounds made by the pennies when they hit the plate are louder than they would be if the pennies were actually placed in the purse, you can place a folded paper napkin or handkerchief on the plate to lessen the sound of the falling coins.)

Snap the purse shut. Pick up the other purse with the right hand. This purse has three pennies concealed in it near the top. Be sure to grip these three coins securely with the right hand before the purse is taken from the pocket.

Display the two purses. Remind the audience that the purse on your left has three dimes and three pennies mixed together.

Swing the two purses toward one another, Figure 169. At the same time, release the three pennies from the right hand's grip. Shake this purse to indicate that it now contains coins. Hand it to a spectator.

Open the purse in your left hand and dump out the three dimes. Allow the spectator to open the other purse and dump out the three pennies.

68. ASTRAL COINS

Two playing cards are shown and placed on the table. The magician places a dime and a penny under the table. The two coins mysteriously penetrate up through the table and appear under the cards. When the coins are covered by the cards, the coins penetrate down through the table.

This routine is based on an idea of the British magician Alex Elmsley.

Method: One end of a short length of fine thread is glued between a dime and a penny. The thread is sandwiched between the coins,

and the coins are glued offset. The other end of the thread is taped
or glued to the center of the back of any ace, Figure 170. A second
playing card is glued face down on top of the first card, Figure 171.
The length of thread between the cards and coins should be about
half the width of a playing card. Also needed is any 10-spot from
the deck.

The two coins hang in back of the ace. The 10-spot is placed in
back of the coins so the coins are between the cards. In this
condition the apparatus is placed in the pocket.

If the reader wishes to try out the routine on an informal basis,
one end of the thread can be taped to the back of a playing card
and the other end taped to a penny or a dollar bill folded in eighths
and pressed flat.

Remove the apparatus from the pocket and hold the cards
upright as indicated in Figure 172. The spectator sees the face of
the ace. The 10-spot in back of the prepared card should be raised
slightly by the thumb as shown in Figure 172.

Turn the apparatus so it rests face up on the table, Figure 173.
Hold the ace in place with the left hand. Slide the 10-spot out with
the right hand.

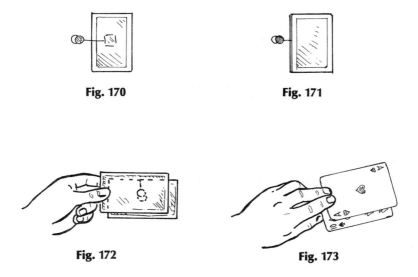

Fig. 170　　　　　　　**Fig. 171**

Fig. 172　　　　　**Fig. 173**

Turn the 10-spot face down. Take it with the left hand and slide it between the coins and the ace, Figure 174. The right fingertips press gently against the ace to keep it in place while the other card is slid under it.

Flip the ace face down by pivoting it toward you, Figure 175. The spectators have thus seen the faces and backs of both cards. The coins remain concealed.

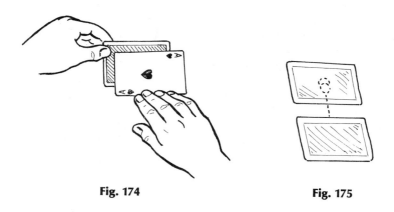

Fig. 174   **Fig. 175**

Flip the ace face up onto the face-down 10-spot. Say, "I use an ace and a ten to match the coins." Remove a duplicate dime and penny from the pocket.

Display the coins. Place them under the table. Rest them on the leg, one coin next to the other, but continue moving the hand under the table so it is directly under the cards.

Rap the hand against the underside of the table. Then turn the two cards over toward you to reveal the two coins, Figure 176. Apparently, the penny and dime penetrated up through the table.

Flip both cards over onto the coins. The apparatus will appear as in Figure 174. Place the left fingertips against the back of the 10-spot to hold it in place. The right hand then slides the ace back toward the body as if to get it away from the other card.

The right hand raises the card to a vertical position so its long edge rests against the table. Unknown to the audience, you have slipped out the two coins behind this card, Figure 177.

Place the right thumb against the coins. Then tap the 10-spot three times with the edge of the ace. At the same time, place the left hand under the table. Pick up the dime and penny from the trouser leg. Tap them three times against the underside of the table.

Flip the 10-spot over with the edge of the ace to show that the coins have vanished. Bring the left hand into view and toss the coins onto the table.

The 10-spot can be placed in back of the ace so the coins are once more concealed between the cards as in Figure 172. The cards are then placed in the pocket. You can have a duplicate unprepared ace in the pocket. At a later time, this ace and the 10-spot can be removed from the pocket.

Perform the trick on a surface covered with a tablecloth. If the thread seems too easily spotted, use a handkerchief with an overall pattern for the working surface.

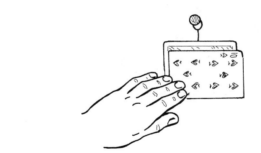

Fig. 176

Fig. 177

69. PUNCTURE

A $10 bill is wrapped in a piece of paper. A pencil is pushed through the paper and bill, Figure 178. The apparatus is shown on both sides. There is no doubt the pencil has torn through the paper and the bill.

When the apparatus is unfolded, it is found that, although the paper has a hole in the center, the bill has restored itself, Figure 179.

Method: This ingenious trick is based on ideas of Murray Sumner, Rick Johnsson and Yoshio Hirose. To prepare, cut a slit near the right side of a play-money $10 bill, Figure 180. The slit should be about ½″ long. This is the extent of the preparation. The bill may be carried in the wallet.

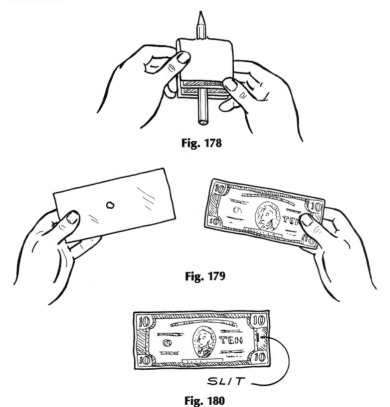

Fig. 178

Fig. 179

SLIT

Fig. 180

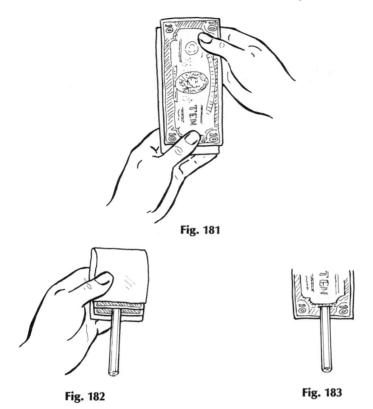

Fig. 181

Fig. 182   Fig. 183

A piece of plain white paper the size of a bill is also required. Place the prepared bill against the paper, with the bill offset about ½″ forward as shown in Figure 181. The left thumb covers the slit in the bill.

Fold the apparatus in half toward you so the bill is on the inside. The ends are slightly offset as shown in Figure 182. Openly insert the point of the pencil between the folds of the bill. Unknown to the audience, the pencil point is actually worked through the slit in the bill. This is shown in the exposed view of Figure 183. Thus the pencil really slides behind the bill.

Continue pushing the pencil forward until it penetrates the center of the paper. When the apparatus is as shown in Figure 178, display it on both sides. It seems beyond doubt that the pencil has torn through the center of the bill.

Remove the pencil. Then open out the apparatus with the paper facing the spectators. From your view the apparatus looks like Figure 181. Take the paper in the left hand, the bill in the right, Figure 179, to reveal that, while there is a hole in the paper, the bill is undamaged. Return the bill to the wallet.

Save this trick for special occasions. It is an impossible-seeming effect that brings gasps of disbelief from spectators.

SHORTCHANGE TRICKS

People benefit from knowing the secrets and methods of confidence men and shortchange artists. Such knowledge arms the public with valuable information on what to look for in their dealings with strangers. This chapter describes three of the best shortchange tricks. If there is a moral that connects these tricks, it is that, when money changes hands with strangers, people should be sure to count their change.

70. BUNCO BILLS

To show how the shortchange artist works, a volunteer spectator makes an imagined $3.75 purchase with a $10 bill. The magician slowly counts his change. All seems fair, but when the count is checked, it is seen the spectator has been shortchanged a dollar.

Method: Needed are five $1 bills. Fold a bill in half in the offset condition shown in Figure 184. Place it second from the bottom of the stack of five bills. This is the only preparation. One or two of the unprepared bills should be face down in the stack.

Fig. 184

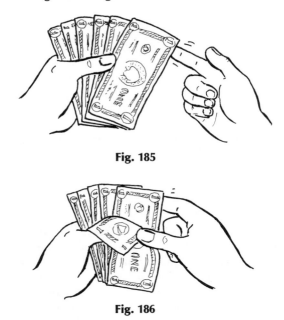

Fig. 185

Fig. 186

Explain that, where large crowds gather, the shortchange artist will ply his trade when someone makes, for example, a $3.75 purchase with a $10 bill. The purchaser should get back $6.25 in change.

Fan the bills as shown in Figure 185. The left thumb hides the folded condition of the bill second from the bottom.

On the count of one, lift the top bill with the right first finger as indicated in Figure 185. Keep this bill isolated from the others by flipping it over the right thumb, Figure 186.

On the count of two, lift the second bill with the right first finger. Flip it over the right thumb. Continue in this way with the remaining bills. Because one bill is folded, it is counted twice. The audience is unaware that you counted five bills as six.

When you have counted the final bill, square up the stack of bills from side to side. Then take the bottom bill with the right hand. Curl the left fingers over the stack, Figure 187. Use these fingers to fold the stack in half. Then place the stack on top of the bill in the right hand and fold this bill in half over the other bills.

Place the folded stack in the spectator's hand. Then give him the remaining 25 cents in change by placing three nickels and a dime

Fig. 187

on top of the folded bills. Explain that by giving the spectator a handful of folded bills and loose change, he has a handful of money and is unlikely to check the count.

It is only later that the spectator realizes he has been short-changed. Have him count the bills in his hand. He should have six but he discovers he has only five. The shortchange artist has made a dollar on the transaction.

71. SHORTCHANGED

Using borrowed money, the magician shows that, even with the money in the spectator's pocket, it is an easy matter to shortchange the unwary.

Fig. 188

Fig. 189

Method: A clever invention of Raymond Beebee is responsible for the working of this routine. Fold a $5 bill in half the long way as shown in Figure 188, with the picture of Lincoln on the inside. Then fold the right half to the left, Figure 189. Fold the right half to the left again as shown by the arrow in Figure 189.

Fig. 190

Fig. 191

Fig. 192

Fold a dollar bill in half the long way, Figure 190, so the picture of Washington is on the inside. Then fold the left half to the right to bring you to the position shown in Figure 191. Fold the left half to the right as shown by the arrow in Figure 191.

Interweave the two folded bills, Figure 192. The result is a packet that looks like a $5 bill on one side and a $1 bill on the other. Place this double bill under a heavy weight overnight to flatten it out. When ready to perform the trick, place the double bill in the right jacket pocket with the $5 side toward the body. The bill should go into the change compartment in the pocket so you can locate it easily later on.

To perform, remark that a shortchange artist once showed you his method of making money. Ask the spectator to remove a $5 bill from his pocket. Remove a $1 bill from your pocket.

The spectator follows with the $5 bill as you fold the $1 bill in eighths. Use the handling described above so each bill is folded with the President's picture on the inside.

Place the $1 bill in your right jacket pocket, toward the front of the pocket. Take the $5 bill from the spectator. Place it in the same pocket, but toward the back of the pocket.

Say, "First you have to learn how to tell one bill from another by sense of touch. That way you don't have to look at the bills when you're handling them." Reach into the pocket. Pause and say, "This should be the $1 bill." Remove the $1 bill from the pocket.

Then reach into the pocket to remove the $5 bill. Actually, you remove the double bill with the $5 side uppermost. Place both bills in the spectator's pocket. Have him mix them. Say, "I can find the

$1 bill by touch." Then reach into his pocket and remove the double bill. Because of the double thickness, you should have no trouble finding this bill by sense of touch. When the double bill is brought into view, make sure the $1 side is uppermost.

Say, "Here's the $1 bill," as you remove the double bill from the spectator's pocket. Place this bill into your right jacket pocket, back into the change compartment.

Start to perform another trick. Then say, "Telling one bill from another is only one thing the shortchange artist does. He wouldn't make money that way. *This* is how he makes his money."

Reach into your jacket pocket. Remove the spectator's $5 bill. The spectator should be surprised that you somehow got his money.

72. BAMBOOZLED

Ideas of Bert Allerton and Dai Vernon are combined in the following routine. The effect is one in which paper money is counted several times. Each time the total is different. Although it appears the magician has been swindled, in the end he comes out ahead of the game.

Method: Use play money for this routine. You will need six $1 bills and two $5 bills. Apply glue or rubber cement to the right half of the front of a $1 bill. The treated portion is shown shaded in Figure 193.

Place a $5 bill on top of the treated $1 bill, Figure 194. The right half of the $5 bill is now pasted or stuck to the right half of the $1 bill. Place this prepared bill on top of a stack of the other $1 bills,

Fig. 193

Fig. 194

Fig. 195

Fig. 196

Figure 195. The open end of the prepared bill is at the bottom. Place the unprepared $5 bill in the trouser pocket.

When presenting the routine, remark that you were once in a nightclub known to be a clip joint. At the end of the meal you asked for change of a $10 bill.

Hold the stack in the left hand. The prepared bill is uppermost. Count the bills from hand to hand one at a time, beginning with the $5 bill, as shown in Figure 196. Count the bills on top of one another. Count out loud, and make sure to count the bills slowly so the audience can follow the action. Say, "The cashier counted a FIVE and five ONES."

Place the stack back into the left hand. Count the bills once more. The stack is back in its original order with the prepared bill on top.

When you complete the count, place the right first finger between the layers of the prepared bill, Figure 197. Then fold the upper half of the stack onto the lower half, Figure 198.

Say, "It looked fair, but as I walked away, I decided to check the count." Allow the right second, third and fourth fingers to release

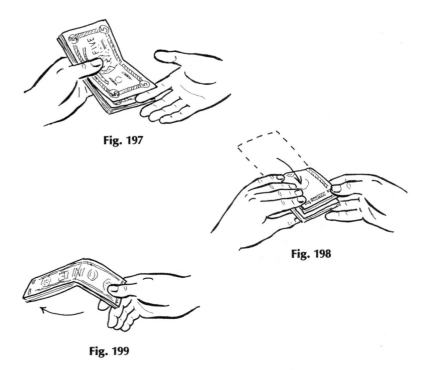

Fig. 197

Fig. 198

Fig. 199

their grip. The stack will open outward as shown in Figure 199. This action turns the stack over. The prepared bill is now on the bottom of the stack, folded.

Count the bills from left to right again, counting the bills one at a time on top of one another. The stack now contains six $1 bills. Say, "I had only six dollars, so I went back to the cashier."

Place the stack in the left hand. As you say, "The cashier counted the bills," count the bills one at a time from hand to hand. The count shows six dollars.

"The cashier apologized. He took a single from the stack and put it in my pocket, saying, 'That is for your trouble.' Then he gave me a fresh $5 bill." Suiting the action to your words, remove the top $1 bill and tuck it into the outer handkerchief pocket of the jacket. Take the $5 bill from the trouser pocket and place it on top of the stack.

"I thanked the cashier for his generosity and left the nightclub." The prepared bill is at the bottom of the stack, folded. Insert the

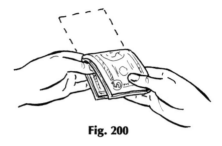

Fig. 200

right first finger into the fold between the layers of the prepared bill. Then fold the outer half of the stack underneath as shown in Figure 200.

"When I told the story, people asked why I thanked the cashier. 'After all,' my friends said, 'he tried to shortchange you.' This is why I thanked him for his generosity."

Release the top half of the stack by taking the right thumb out of the way. The stack will open out flat with the prepared bill on top. Place the stack in the left hand.

Slowly count the bills from left to right. You will now have $14. Add the dollar bill from your handkerchief pocket, saying, "And this makes fifteen dollars. I may go back to that club again sometime!"

MONEY MENTAL

"Almost everyone seems to have had some kind of extrasensory experience that cannot be explained," Milbourne Christopher observed. The magician who makes it appear that he can read the future or tune in on thought waves will always get an enthusiastic reaction from audiences. The tricks in this chapter center around psychic magic performed with coins and bills.

73. DIVINATION

Three pairs of coins are hidden under three playing cards. The apparatus is mixed about. Although the coins are hidden under the cards, the magician succeeds in revealing where the various coins are.

Method: Ron Edwards developed this routine. Needed are three nickels, three pennies and three playing cards. The cards are a 2, a 6 and a 10. The cards must be secretly marked on the back. The 2 can be marked with one pencil dot, the 6 with two dots and the 10 with three dots.

To present the trick, put the coins down on the table in pairs, two nickels together, two pennies together in another pile and six cents (nickel plus penny) in a third pile.

Tell the spectator the 10-spot is to indicate the two nickels, the 2-spot the two pennies, and the 6-spot the penny-and-nickel combination. In other words, each card reflects the total of two coins.

Turn your back. Have the spectator mix around the pairs of coins, leaving them in the same combinations, but in different locations on the table. When he has done this, ask him to turn the playing cards face up and cover the three sets of coins. He is to place the 2-spot on the two-cent pile, the 6-spot on the six-cent pile and the 10-spot on the ten-cent pile.

Now tell him, "To confuse the situation further, shift the position of the three cards so the card values do not match up with any of the money combinations they cover." When the spectator has done this, say, "And to add further confusion, please turn each card face down in place."

Turn around. Secretly spot the pencil dots so you know where the 6-spot is. Ask the spectator to hand you one of the coins from under it. If it is the penny, you know the two nickels are under the 2-spot and the six cents are under the 10-spot.

If the coin removed by the spectator is a nickel, you know the two pennies are under the 10-spot and the six cents are under the 2-spot. In either case, pretend to receive the necessary mental vibrations from the coin handed to you. Then reveal the whereabouts of the other coins.

74. TIME WILL TELL

Twelve coins are arranged like a clock dial. A key is placed in the center, the top of the key pointing to the 12-o'clock position. The spectator turns over six coins randomly.

The magician, his back turned, has the spectator remove six coins and slide them to one side. It is found that the number of heads and tails showing on these six coins exactly matches the other six coins.

No questions are asked. The magician never knows which six coins were turned over by the spectator.

Method: This subtle trick was devised by Bob Hummer and Jack Yates. Arrange 12 coins to represent a clock dial. All coins are heads up. A key is placed in the center as in Figure 201, the top of the key pointing to the 12-o'clock position. A toothpick or other similarly shaped object may be used in place of the key. The key acts as a reference point so the 12-o'clock position is clearly marked.

Fig. 201

Turn your back. Have the spectator turn over any six coins in place. When he has finished, there will be six coins with heads showing, six with tails showing.

Ask the spectator to turn over the coins at positions 2, 4, 6, 8, 10, 12 on the clock face. Explain that this further randomizes the distribution of heads and tails.

Then have him remove the coins at positions 1, 3, 5, 7, 9, 11. These coins are slid away from the clock face without being turned over, and placed in a separate group on the table.

Say, "If I can tell psychic time correctly, I should have divided up the coins so that each group shows the same number of heads, and each group shows the same number of tails."

Turn and face the audience. Let the assisting spectator verify that you did indeed divide the coins into two equal groups of heads and tails.

The trick works just as described above. If you wish to disguise the principle, proceed as follows.

After the spectator has turned over six coins randomly, say to him, "Turn over the coin at position 1, the coin at position 10, the coins at positions 2 and 8 and the coins at positions 4 and 5." Say this slowly, allowing the spectator time to suit his actions to your instructions.

When he has done this, say, "Now remove the coins at the position a quarter after nine [he would remove the coins at positions 3 and 9], the coins at position seven-thirty [he would remove the coins at positions 6 and 7] and the coins at position five to midnight [he would remove the coins at positions 11 and 12]."

Before telling him to remove the coins, make it clear he is to remove them by sliding them to another location on the table away from the clock face, and that he is not to turn them over.

If the above instruction is followed correctly, each group of six coins will have the same number of heads and tails showing. The routine can be done over the telephone.

75. TAKE ONE

On the table are a quarter, a half-dollar and a silver dollar. Each of three spectators takes one of these coins and hides it in his hand. The magician's back has been turned until this point.

The magician faces the three spectators and reveals who took which coin. No questions are asked. The trick may be repeated. This clever routine was originated by the British magician Al Koran.

Method: The first spectator is a confederate. The first time the trick is done, he takes the quarter. The second spectator takes either the half-dollar or the dollar. As soon as the confederate sees the second spectator's choice, he proceeds as follows.

If the second spectator took the dollar, the confederate places his coin in his right hand. Otherwise he places his coin in his left hand.

The spectators are instructed to hide the coins by placing them behind their backs. Turn and face the second spectator. Out of the corner of your eye you can tell if the confederate's right or left hand is behind his back. If his right hand is behind his back, the second spectator took the dollar. If this is the case, you would say to the second spectator, "I had a hunch you'd go for the big money. You chose the silver dollar."

Go on from here to reveal the coin held by the third spectator, then the coin held by the confederate.

If the trick is repeated, the confederate is to pick the half-dollar. The presentation is otherwise the same, i.e., if the second spectator chooses the dollar, the confederate places his own coin in his right hand. Otherwise he places the half-dollar in his left hand.

76.   DESTINY

Based on an idea of Vic Shoenk's, this is an exceptional magic trick. Several coins are tossed onto the table. The spectator chooses any coin. He shuffles a deck of cards, then deals the cards into four rows on the table.

The date on the coin is noted. Say it is 1989. The four packets are turned over. The face cards have the numbers 1, 9, 8, 9, exactly matching the date on the chosen coin.

Method: A penny, nickel, dime and quarter are used. All four coins have the same date. Say this date is 1989. Place the coins in the left jacket pocket.

Remove an ace, 9, 8 and 9 from a deck of cards. Slide them under the clip of a pen and place the clipped packet face out in the upper handkerchief pocket of the jacket, Figure 202. This completes the preparation.

Hand the balance of the deck out for shuffling. When the spectator is satisfied the cards are well mixed, take back the deck in the right hand. Make sure the first and second fingers are at the front of the pack.

With the left hand remove the coins from the pocket and place them in the spectator's hand. Tell him to mix the coins and choose one.

As he does this, bring the right hand to the outer handkerchief pocket and clip the pen between the right first and second fingers,

Fig. 202

Fig. 203

Figure 203. Slide the pen and the clipped packet of cards upward and out of the pocket. The packet of four cards is thus added to the top of the deck.

With the left hand slide the pen free from the cards. Hand it to the spectator. Take back the three coins not chosen and return them to the pocket. Have the spectator jot down on a piece of paper the date on the chosen coin.

Hand the deck to the spectator. Ask him to deal it into four heaps. He can stop the deal at any time. He announces the date he chose. Then he turns up the four heaps to discover that the face cards match the chosen date.

77. METALOGIC

"I have here some fine portraits of U.S. Presidents," the performer says. As he talks, he places a penny, a nickel, a dime and a quarter on the table. "Washington is on the quarter, Roosevelt on the dime, Jefferson on the nickel and Lincoln on the penny," the performer explains.

Turning his back, he says, "I'd like you to choose one of the coins. Hold it in your hand so you can see the portrait of the President. Cover the other three coins with a piece of paper."

His back still turned, the magician now reveals which President the spectator is looking at. Nothing is written down. The magician may be blindfolded. The trick is impromptu and can be done at any time.

Method: This offbeat trick is based on a principle developed by Edward Bagshawe and Sam Schwartz. The present version was devised by the author. For the trick to work, all you need remember are the letters *n-i-l*, in that order.

Place the four coins heads up on the table. Turn your back. Have the spectator choose a coin and place it heads up on his palm. Have him cover the other three coins.

Close your eyes and pretend to think psychic thoughts. Then say, "The President you are looking at—his name contains the letter *n*." If the spectator says no, reply, "I meant that his first name, Franklin, contains two *n*'s. He's a modern-day President. Roosevelt, correct?" You will be correct.

If the spectator says yes to *n*, say, "There's also an *i*." If the spectator says no, reply, "I meant that you see only one eye because he's in profile. It's President Jefferson, correct?" You will be correct.

If the spectator says yes to *i*, say, "I see what looks like an *l*." If the spectator says no to *l*, reply, "Now that I think of it, that *l* is really the number one, which stands for our first President, George Washington, correct?" You will be correct.

If the spectator says yes to *l*, say, "The letters *n*, *i*, *l* are really the first three letters of his name in reverse order. That should be *L-i-n* for Lincoln, correct?" You will be correct.

Note that, in the above series of statements, as soon as you get your first no answer, you know the name of the chosen President.

78. IMMOVABLE OBJECT

While the magician turns his back, a spectator drops a coin into any one of six numbered glasses, Figure 204. At the magician's direction the spectator moves the coin from glass to glass. The glasses are eliminated one at a time until only one glass remains. Remarkably, it is the glass that contains the coin, and the number on the glass matches a previously written prediction.

Fig. 204

This brilliant trick is based on ideas of Bob Hummer, Stewart James and Mel Stover. The magician can be in the next room. There are no gimmicks or confederates. The magician never knows the location of the coin until the very end, yet the prediction is always correct.

Method: Use six numbered glasses like those shown in Figure 204. The glasses can be numbered by placing adhesive labels on them and numbering the labels. On a piece of paper write, "No matter what you do, Fate has decreed the coin will end up in glass No. 5." Fold the paper and place it in plain view on the table.

Turn your back or leave the room. Ask the spectator to place the coin in any glass. When he has done so, ask him to note the number of the glass and to make that number of moves. A move consists of pouring the coin from its glass into an adjacent glass.

If the coin is in glass No. 3 at the start, for example, the spectator would make three moves. If the coin is in glass No. 6 at the start, the spectator would make six moves.

When he has done this, ask him to remove glass No. 1.

Have him make one move. Then ask him to remove glass No. 6.

Have the spectator make four moves. Then tell him to remove glass No. 2.

Let him make three moves. Then have him remove glass No. 3.

Finally, have him make three more moves and remove glass No. 4.

The coin will be in glass No. 5, matching the prediction exactly.

A LESSON IN TIMING

Jean Hugard once wrote that "The fundamental basis of magic with coins is the art of palming, that is, of holding and concealing a coin or several coins, in the palm of one hand, while pretending to place them in the other."

Because palming is fundamental to money magic, a book on the subject would not be complete without mention of palming. Coin expert Bill Wisch has developed a nearly self-working method of mastering the classic palm using the technique of timing. If you follow the Bill Wisch instructions given here, and if you can count to three, you can perform a deceptive classic palm the first time you try it.

79. EASY AS 1, 2, 3

The Bill Wisch technique uses a system of beats to perform the palm. The idea is to tap the foot rhythmically to establish the beats. Use a slow rhythm when learning the move. Gradually increase the tempo to a point where it feels comfortable and looks natural.

In this first sequence, the coin will actually be transferred from the left hand to the right. This is to establish the way the handling would look if the coin was actually transferred from hand to hand. A dollar bill folded in eighths may be used in place of a coin. Some people may find this easier because the sharp edges of a folded bill make it easy to grip.

On the count of one, the coin is in the position shown in Figure 205. The right hand is palm up. The coin rests on the right palm. The left first finger points to the coin. The tip of the left first finger contacts the coin.

On the count of two, the hands have moved to the position shown in Figure 206. The coin has been dropped into the left palm. The edge of the right hand touches the base of the left fingers.

The count of three is shown in Figure 207. The left fingers have closed around the coin and the right hand has been lifted out of the way. This completes the basic action. Remember to maintain a steady tempo. On the counts of one, two, three, you will arrive at, respectively, the positions shown in Figures 205, 206, 207.

When performing the classic palm, the hands should appear to go through the same actions. On the count of one, the coin is in the position shown in Figure 205. To check that the position is correct, if you move the right thumb slightly to the left, the coin will be gripped between the base of the thumb and the palm, Figure 208. The right fingers do not move. With the coin gripped as in Figure 208, you should be able to turn the hand palm down and retain the coin in position. The left first finger can aid by pushing the coin down into the right palm in Figure 205.

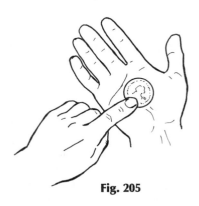

Fig. 205

Fig. 206

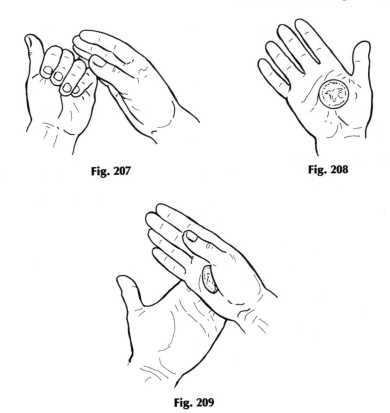

Fig. 207 **Fig. 208**

Fig. 209

On the count of two, the hands have reached the position of Figure 209. The coin is gripped in classic palm position in the right hand. The back of the right hand is toward the spectators, concealing the true situation from audience view.

On the count of three, the left fingers close and the right hand moves to the position of Figure 207. This completes the pretended placement of the coin into the left hand.

If you wish to show that the coin has vanished, on the count of four you can open the left hand to show the hand empty.

If you have trouble gripping the coin as shown in Figure 208, the coin may be the wrong size. Try palming with a larger or smaller coin or with a folded dollar bill. If the hands are dry, the coin will slip; use a hand lotion to moisten the hands.

80.   COIN THRU TABLE

This is an application of the Bill Wisch classic palm in which a borrowed coin penetrates the table.

On the count of one, display the coin as in Figure 205. On the count of two, pretend to drop the coin into the left palm, Figure 209. On the count of three, close the left hand and bring the right hand to the position shown in Figure 207.

Place the closed left hand palm down on the tabletop. At the same time, place the right hand palm down on the right leg. Leave the palmed coin on the leg.

Raise the right hand. With the palm toward the audience, snap the fingers. Say, "It's important to do that or the trick won't work." The audience has a chance to see that the right hand is empty.

Bring the right hand under the table. Pick up the coin with the right fingers. Rap the left fist against the table once or twice. Then open the hand and slap it palm down against the table.

Turn the left hand palm up to show that the coin has vanished. At the same time, bring the right hand up into view, displaying the coin at the fingertips.

Any small, easily palmed object, such as a book of matches, may be used in place of the coin.

HAUNTED HOUSE

Periodically, television and newspapers will feature news stories of people who claim to have had psychic experiences. John Mulholland, a skeptic on the subject, nevertheless recommended psychic themes as a marvelous way to establish a spooky atmosphere for the demonstration of magical effects.

The tricks in this chapter are based on the premise that the apparatus was discovered in a haunted house. Odd-looking coins can be obtained at antique shops. The boxes and glasses used in these tricks can be painted to appear antique. Such apparatus adds to the atmosphere of the magic.

81. THRU AND THRU

Two opaque plastic drinking glasses are used for an offbeat trick devised by Roy Walton. The glasses are placed mouth up on the table. A coin is then dropped into one glass. This glass is held by the left hand.

The other glass is lifted to a position over the first glass, Figure 210. The magician says, "One glass is real, the other only a ghost of a glass. It passes right through the solid glass." The upper glass is released and immediately penetrates the glass in the left hand.

The coin is then poured out of the left-hand glass. The visible penetration may be repeated.

Fig. 210

Method: Secretly place a coin in an opaque plastic glass. Then nest another glass in this one. The glasses may be carried in this condition until the time of performance.

When ready to perform, place the nested glasses on the table. Lift out the upper glass. Drop a duplicate coin into it. Hold this glass near the rim with the left hand about 8″ above the table.

Pick up the other glass by grasping it at the rim with the right hand. Take care not to rattle the coin in this glass. You want the audience to think the glass is empty.

Place this glass over the glass in the left hand, Figure 210. Release the upper glass. It will drop into the lower glass. If the left hand has a light grip on its glass, the impact of the upper glass dropping into the lower glass will cause the lower glass to fall onto the table. The left hand will now hold the upper glass.

Properly performed, the illusion is that the upper glass penetrated the lower glass and dropped onto the table. The illusion is made perfect by the fact that after the glass drops onto the table, the left hand pours a coin out of its glass.

To finish, drop the empty glass into the other glass and place both glasses aside.

82. REBOUND

A silver coin is wrapped in a piece of paper and placed in an envelope. A copper coin is dropped into the envelope. The magician snaps his fingers. The folded paper is removed and opened to reveal that now the copper coin is in the paper. The silver coin is then removed from the envelope.

There are no extra coins or gimmicks. The silver coin is inside the paper right up to the instant that the paper is removed from the envelope.

Method: This routine was devised by the author. The paper measures about 5½″ × 4″. The envelope is the end-opening type. It measures about 3½″ × 3″.

The folded paper can be kept inside the envelope. Remark that this is all that remains of a transaction that took place a century ago, in which someone sent money in the mail to purchase a rare coin. The mails operated more efficiently back then.

Place the silver coin at a point about ½″ below the center of the paper. Hold the coin in place with the left thumb, Figure 211. The lower left corner of the paper is marked with an X as a reference point for the reader.

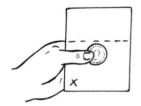

Fig. 211

Fold the upper part of the paper down on top of the coin, so the edge is about ½″ above the bottom of the paper.

Then fold the right side of the paper over to the left, Figure 212. Fold the left side over to the right, Figure 213. Turn the paper over end for end (*not* side for side). This brings the corner marked X to the top as shown in Figure 214.

The protruding ½″ at the top is now folded down toward you. The completed fold looks as shown in Figure 215. The coin appears to be trapped inside the paper. Unknown to the audience, the top of the paper is open.

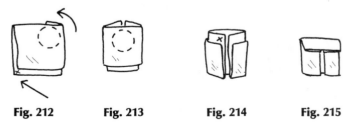

Fig. 212   **Fig. 213**   **Fig. 214**   **Fig. 215**

Fig. 216

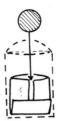

Fig. 217

Turn the envelope around end for end to the position shown in Figure 216. Then place the folded paper into the envelope. Maintain pressure on the coin until the folded paper rests securely on the bottom of the envelope. Remark that this was how that person in the distant past mailed out payment for the rare coin.

Display the copper coin, calling it the rare coin that was purchased. Drop it into the envelope, but make sure it slides into the folded paper as indicated by the arrow in Figure 217. The fingers of the hand holding the envelope can buckle the sides of the envelope to make this easier.

Say, "Here's how quickly this fellow got the rare coin." Snap the fingers. Reach into the envelope and remove the paper package, Figure 218. The silver coin automatically remains in the envelope.

Place the envelope on the table. Holding the copper coin in place concealed behind the paper, unfold the bottom and side flaps of the paper. Then pretend to dump the copper coin onto the table.

Say, "And the coin dealer got his money." Tip the envelope to allow the silver coin to drop to the table.

The transposition can be done between such dissimilar objects as a coin and a key or a coin and a poker chip.

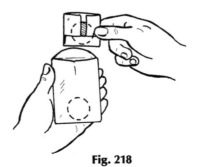

Fig. 218

83. THE GATHERING

The magician reenacts a card game from bygone days in which one fellow's bet mysteriously ended up in the other fellow's possession. As the audience sees it, a coin is covered with a playing card. Another card is placed on the table. The coin vanishes from under the first card and appears under the second. The effect is immediately repeated with a second coin.

Method: A prepared card is used. Trim about ¼″ from one long side of a playing card, cutting away the portion shown by the dotted lines in Figure 219. Then glue an unprepared card on top of this card. Glue is applied as shown by the shaded lines in Figure 220. You have thus formed a pocket card.

Fig. 219   **Fig. 220**

Place four quarters in a group on the table. Closer to you and to the left place the pocket card. The opening of the pocket is toward you. Place an unprepared playing card to the right of the pocket card. The layout is shown in Figure 221. The pocket card is at *A*, the unprepared card at *B*. Both cards are face down. The trick should be performed on a soft surface like a tablecloth.

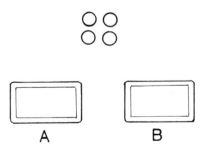

A   B

Fig. 221

Remark that you found the cards and coins just like this on a table in a haunted house. A card game was in progress. You will try to reenact the game as you think it progressed.

Take one of the quarters with the right hand. The left hand grasps the pocket card from above. The thumb lifts the near edge of the upper card. Pretend to place the quarter under this card. Actually, insert it into the pocket, Figure 222.

Pick up another quarter. Place it under the card at position *B*. Remark that the bets were covered with cards, and that the players had the option of trading cards. Grasp the card at *A* with the left hand. Grasp the card at *B* with the right hand.

Place the right-hand card on top of the left-hand card, Figure 223. Slide the left-hand card to the left. Then release the right-hand card. The audience assumes that this card now covers the coin on the left.

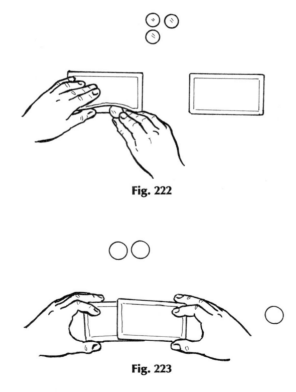

Fig. 222

Fig. 223

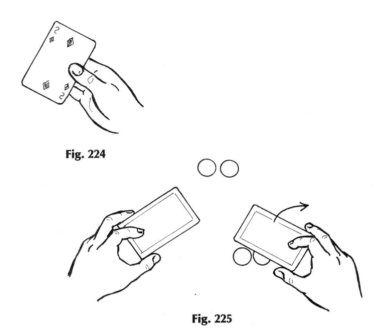

Fig. 224

Fig. 225

The palm-down right hand now grasps the pocket card at the center. Turn the card face up, Figure 224, then turn the card face down and place it on top of the coin on the right.

Snap the fingers. Say, "I don't know the rules of the game, but this fellow won." Lift the card at A to show that the coin has vanished. Grasp the pocket card with the right hand. Tilt the front end of this card up so the coin will slide out of the pocket. At the same time, pivot the pocket card to the right, Figure 225, to reveal that there are now two coins before the winning player on the right.

Repeat the effect with the remaining two coins. At the finish, drop the cards into the jacket pocket to get rid of the evidence.

84. SEALED-BOX MYSTERY

A cardboard matchbox is shown empty and placed on the table. A coin is placed under the table. Immediately, the coin penetrates the table and appears inside the matchbox. The trick may be repeated.

Method: This is a new handling of a classic trick. Beforehand, place a coin like a quarter on the inside bottom of the matchbox. Close the drawer or tray so it rides over the coin, Figure 226. The coin is now trapped between the drawer and the box. It will remain in this position until you are ready to perform the routine. You can have a few matches in the drawer.

To perform the routine, slide the drawer out with the left hand. Grasp the box between the right thumb and fingers, Figure 227. The thumb goes directly on top of the quarter. The right hand is palm up.

Pull the drawer clear of the box. Show the box and drawer on both sides. Unknown to the audience, there is a quarter inside the box, held in place with the right thumb.

Turn the right hand palm down. Slide the drawer back into the box, Figure 228. The quarter will end up trapped between the top

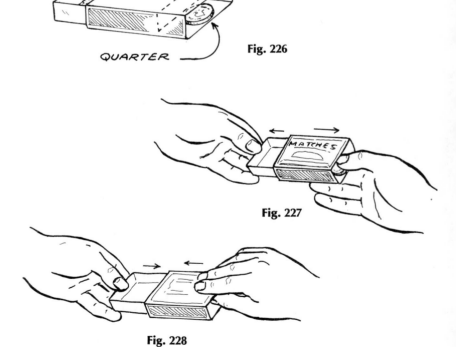

QUARTER

Fig. 226

Fig. 227

Fig. 228

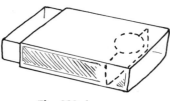

Fig. 229-A   **Fig. 229-B**

edge of the drawer and the top of the box, Figure 229-A. It will remain in this position as long as the drawer is in the partially open position shown in Figure 229-A.

Show a duplicate quarter. Place it under the table. Drop it into the shoe or leave it in the lap. As the right hand goes under the table, the left hand grasps the matchbox, fingers at the left side, thumb at the right side.

The right hand raps against the underside of the table. At the same time the left hand taps the matchbox against the table and closes the drawer. The result is that the quarter will fall into the matchbox with an audible clink. The illusion is that the quarter penetrated up through the table and landed inside the matchbox with a loud clink.

There is a little-known repeat version of the trick. To begin, place one coin on the bottom of the box as shown in Figure 226. Slide the drawer into the box until it is almost flush. Then slide another quarter between the drawer and the top of the box as shown in Figure 229-B.

Place the box on the table. Display another coin (a third quarter) and place it under the table. Remark that the box represents a locked room in the house and the quarter a ghost. You are going to demonstrate how the ghost manages to materialize in the locked room.

When the right hand is under the table, tuck the quarter into the sock. Rap the right hand against the bottom of the table. At the same time, close the box with the left hand. The result is that the quarter trapped between the drawer and the box will fall into the box.

With the box kept on the table, open the box to show the quarter. Dump the quarter onto the table. Now grasp the box as shown in Figure 227. The right thumb goes on top of the coin that is still inside the box. Pull the drawer clear of the box with the right hand.

Then show the box and drawer on both sides. Replace the drawer in the box as in Figure 228. Then go on with the rest of the handling as described above. For patter, say that you will show once more how the ghost gets into the locked room.

85. HOLED OUT

This is a modernized version of an old puzzle in which you demonstrate how to push a coin through a hole that is smaller than the coin. First you perform the classic method of working a coin through a hole slightly smaller than the diameter of the coin. Then you cause the coin to slide visibly through a hole that is *much* smaller than the coin.

Method: The routine is based on ideas of John Howie and the author. It uses one piece of paper and one coin. In the following description it will be assumed that a half-dollar is the coin you will use.

The paper measures 6″ × 4½″. The upper hole, labeled A in Figure 230, is just slightly smaller than a half-dollar. The other hole, labeled B, is smaller than A, measuring less than ¾″ in diameter.

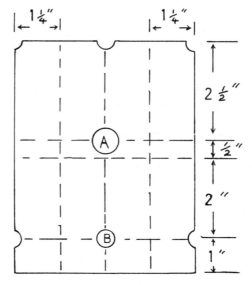

Fig. 230

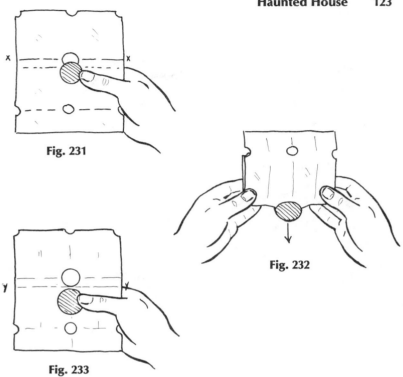

Fig. 231

Fig. 232

Fig. 233

The semicircular cutouts around the border correspond in size to circle *B*. Fold the paper along the dotted lines to complete the preparation.

Display the paper and the half-dollar. Place the coin against circle *A*, Figure 231. Fold the paper down along the upper dotted line *X–X* so the coin is inside the paper. Turn the paper over end for end and hold it as shown in Figure 232. Make it clear that the circular cutout is smaller than the coin. Ask the spectator if he can get the coin to slide through the hole in the paper without tearing the paper.

The solution is to grip the paper as in Figure 232. Bend the sides upward. This has the effect of widening the hole enough for the coin to fall through.

Now offer to try the more difficult task of causing the coin to fall through the smaller hole *B*. Place the coin just below hole *A*, Figure 233. Fold the upper part of the paper down over the coin along the

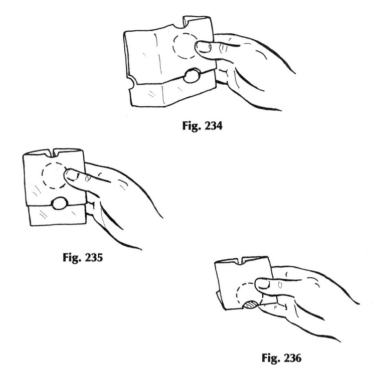

Fig. 234

Fig. 235

Fig. 236

dotted lines just above the coin, shown as X–X in Figure 233. Fold the right side around in front, Figure 234.

Fold the left side around in front, Figure 235. Then fold the bottom portion around in front. This brings you to the situation shown in Figure 236. Allow the coin to slide to the position shown in Figure 236. The apparatus may be shown on both sides. It seems clearly impossible to get the half-dollar through the small hole.

Grasp the coin, pretend to tug on it, then pull it clear of the paper. Unfold the paper by starting at the position of Figure 236 and working back to Figure 233.

By way of patter, remark that you found a worn piece of paper and an ancient coin in a haunted house. The coin seemed to have the ability to change its size. Then go on to demonstrate the above routine.

86.   COINS AND CUPS

Two paper cups and eight coins are used to reenact a classic mystery. Four coins are placed in each cup. One at a time, the coins invisibly leave one cup and appear in the other.

Method: The paper cups should measure about 5″ in height. One of them is prepared by cutting a slot in the base. The slot should be just wide enough so the coin will protrude from the slot without sliding completely through. If half-dollars are used, the slot should measure slightly more than an inch across.

Also needed are nine identical coins. Place one in the unprepared cup. Nest the prepared cup inside it, then drop the other eight coins inside the prepared cup.

When presenting the routine, grasp both cups and pour the eight coins out onto the table. Place the nested cups mouth up on the table. Make sure the slot in the prepared cup is positioned at the back, that is, away from the spectators.

Pick up the prepared cup with the right hand. Tip the mouth slightly back toward you. Drop in a coin, counting, "One." This coin will protrude through the slot when it hits the bottom of the cup. Hold it in place by pressure of the right thumb, Figure 237.

Count three more coins into the cup. Then pick up the other four coins with the left hand. Count them aloud as you pick them up. Drop them together into the unprepared cup.

Hold a cup in each hand. Give them a shake. Then tip the right-hand cup down and allow three coins to fall out. The thumb retains the fourth coin in the slot. Make sure you keep the mouth of the cup away from the audience to keep them from seeing into the cup.

Fig. 237

Pour the coins out of the left-hand cup. Place this cup down. Use the left hand to count these five coins into the prepared cup. Release the right thumb's grip on the coin in the slot. Then pour all the coins from this cup into the unprepared cup. Unknown to the audience, there are now six coins in the unprepared cup.

Repeat the same procedure so that the second and third coins apparently pass from one cup to another. At this point there will be eight coins in the unprepared cup. The audience thinks there are seven.

Pick up the last coin on the table and place it in your pocket. Snap the fingers. Then pour the coins out of the unprepared cup into the hand. Count them one at a time back into the cup to show that the eighth coin has vanished from the pocket and has appeared in the cup.

PLATFORM TRICKS

Coins and bills are used in every type of show, whether it be a close-up performance or a platform act. The tricks in this chapter have been used by professional magicians for the entertainment of audiences large and small. The chapter closes with a trick that uses the book you are now reading.

87. THE MISER'S DREAM

The trick in which the magician plucks a seemingly endless number of coins from thin air was known as "The Ariel Treasury" in Robert Houdin's time. As a feature trick in the stage act of T. Nelson Downs, it gained great popularity. The following is one of the simplest methods of performing this classic feat.

Method: Use a kraft paper bag that measures about 4″ × 7″ on the bottom and is about 12″ in height. These dimensions are not crucial. You want a paper bag that can be easily handled.

Fold back the rim about 2″. Place the bag mouth down on the table. Put three half-dollars into the folded portion, Figure 238.

Fig. 238

The bag is kept in this condition until the performance. The coins are at the back of the bag and are thus concealed from audience view.

To perform the trick, grasp the bag from above with the palm-down right hand. Lift the bag off the table. Then grasp the rim of the bag at the back where the coins are, using the palm-up left hand. The left thumb keeps the coins in place. Turn the bag mouth up.

Look into the air above your head as if searching for an invisible coin floating in the air. Rest the bottom of the bag on the palm-up right hand. Silently release one coin by easing pressure and allowing the coin to drop. The coin falls into the right palm, Figure 239.

Reach into the air with the right hand. Push the coin to the fingertips as you do this so it appears you have plucked a coin from the air. Display the coin and drop it into the bag.

Rattle the bag with the left hand. Rest the bag on the right palm, but do not release another coin. Look to the right, then to the left. As you do this, place the left third finger over on top of the second finger, Figure 240. This action is hidden because the left hand is inside the bag.

When you look to the left, do a double take and look back to the right. Extend the bag in the air as if to catch another coin. As you do, release the left third finger by snapping it against the bag. This will produce a sharp sound as if another coin fell into the bag.

Place the bag on the right palm. Peer down into the bag as if you yourself are amazed that another coin appeared from nowhere. As you do this, allow another coin to fall into the right palm as in Figure 239.

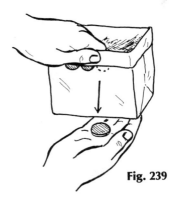

Fig. 239

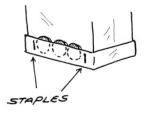

Fig. 240   **Fig. 241**

Produce this coin as you did the first one. Drop it into the bag. Then repeat the action shown in Figure 240. Pantomime catching another coin by the action of extending the bag and making the snapping sound with the finger.

Finally, release the last coin as in Figure 239. Produce it at the fingertips and drop it into the bag.

If you find the pocket is loose and does not retain the coins neatly, use staples to tighten the pocket, Figure 241. This will aid in keeping the coins in place.

88.   HYPER BANKING

In the future, banking will be done in higher dimensions. To illustrate, the magician deposits a coin into a slot in a piece of cardboard, Figure 242. The coin vanishes into hyperspace.

Fig. 242

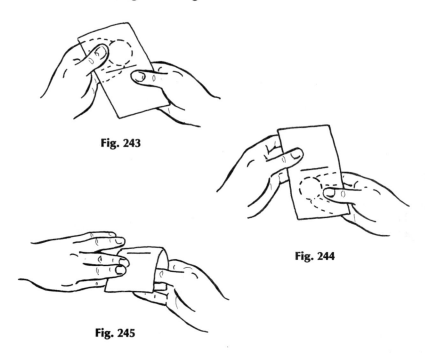

Fig. 243

Fig. 244

Fig. 245

Method: You will need a piece of cardboard measuring about 6″ × 3½″. If cardboard is not available, a blank postcard of similar size may be used. A slot about 1¾″ wide is cut in the center of the cardboard.

Hold the cardboard in the left hand. Slide a half-dollar into the slot, Figure 242. The left first finger behind the cardboard pulls the coin up until the coin is completely through the slot, Figure 243.

The left first finger then slides the coin down behind the cardboard. The coin is gripped by the right first finger and pulled down below the slot, Figure 244.

The left hand turns the top half of the cardboard over to show that the coin has vanished, Figure 245. Bend the cardboard without creasing it. The cardboard is then straightened out to the position shown in Figure 244.

The coin is then transferred back to the left first finger, Figure 243. At this point, the right hand can bend the lower half of the cardboard upward to show again that the coin is gone.

Straighten out the cardboard. Slide the coin back into view as shown in Figure 242. Patter is to the effect that a deposit made here can end up in some other part of the world. If the depositor gets nervous about his money, he can always bring it back.

"Hyper Banking" is based on an ingenious routine invented by the British magician E. Brian MacCarthy.

89. COIN-JURING

A coin is tossed upward. It vanishes into thin air. When the coin is caught in a hat, it drops through the hat and comes to rest in a drinking glass.

All props may be borrowed. Only the visible apparatus is used. There are no gimmicks.

Method: This routine is based on ideas of Al Lasher and the author. Required are a hat that has a hatband, a drinking glass and a coin. The coin can be a half-dollar, a silver dollar or a poker chip.

Display the coin and slip it into the hatband, Figure 246. Show the glass to the audience, then place it mouth up on the table near the hat.

Pretend to take the coin with the right hand. Actually, the right thumb pushes the coin all the way down into the band so the coin is completely concealed from audience view, Figure 247.

Lift the hand as if it contained the coin. Pantomime tossing the coin into the air. Pretend to follow its flight by looking upward. Smile as you do this, as if pleased with the trajectory of the coin.

Fig. 246

Fig. 247

Fig. 248

Allow the smile to fade slowly as you realize the coin has vanished into thin air. Stare upward. Then smile again, as if you have spotted the invisible coin.

Turn the hat brim upward. Hold the hat over the glass. Pretend to catch the coin in the hat. Look down into the hat and smile in a satisfied way, as if the coin has been caught successfully. At the same time, lower the hat sharply against the glass, Figure 248. This jars the coin loose, causing it to fall into the glass.

Pick up the glass and rattle it to emphasize the location of the coin, and take your bow.

90.   A STAB IN THE PACK

A randomly chosen card is returned to the deck. The deck is wrapped with a dollar bill and a rubber band. The magician picks up a knife and inserts the knife blade into the center of the pack. The deck is parted at that point. It is discovered that the knife has found the chosen card.

Method: The invention of Al Koran, this famous trick uses a dollar bill as a kind of visible index; the bill indicates where the deck should be stabbed to find the chosen card.

Jog the card that lies twentieth from the top of the deck. Place a dollar bill on top of the deck, then wrap it around the deck as shown in Figure 249. Use a crisp new bill and make the creases sharp. Indicate with a pencil mark the location of the jogged card. The pencil mark is shown by the arrow in Figure 249.

Remove the dollar bill from the deck. Fold it carefully along the creases. Deal the top 20 cards of the deck into a pile on the table. Place the folded dollar bill on top of the pile. Then place the rest of the deck on top. Snap a rubber band around the deck. This completes the preparation.

When presenting the trick, remove the rubber band and place the deck on the table. Lift off about a third of the deck. Have the spectator shuffle this packet and remove a card. He initials the face of the card and places the initialed card on top of the packet.

The packet is replaced on top of the deck. Spread the deck from hand to hand until you get to the dollar bill. Cut the deck at that point and complete the cut. As you go through these actions, say, "This trick cost me a dollar to perform. Here's the dollar."

Wrap the dollar around the deck, using the folded creases as a guide. The creases must line up exactly with the edges of the deck just as they did in the preliminary preparation of Figure 249. Snap the rubber band around the deck.

Hold the deck in one hand, table knife in the other. Stab the knife into the deck at exactly the point indicated by the pencil mark, Figure 250. If you twist the knife blade a bit after it is in the deck, the deck will open up slightly. Catch the reflection in the knife blade to spot the identity of the card above the knife.

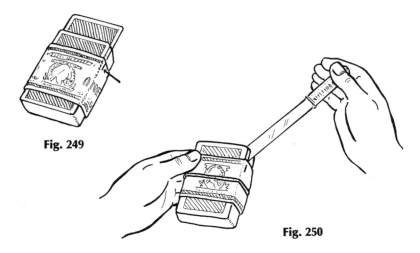

Fig. 249

Fig. 250

Leave the knife in the deck as you remove the rubber band and the dollar bill. Then lift up the cards above the knife. As you do this, ask for the name of the chosen card. If care was taken when the bill was wrapped around the deck, and if the knife was stabbed into the pack at the exact point indicated by the pencil mark, the chosen card will be either directly above or below the knife blade.

You know the name of the face card of the upper packet by spotting its reflection in the knife blade. If this is the chosen card, turn the upper packet over to show that the face card is the chosen card. Otherwise turn over the top card of the lower packet to reveal it as the chosen card.

In the original routine, Al Koran used distinguishing marks in the printing on a borrowed bill as a guide to line up the bill correctly when it was wrapped around the deck. Another distinguishing mark in the printing on the bill indicated the point at which the knife was to be stabbed into the pack. The reader may wish to familiarize himself with such marks so a borrowed bill can be employed in the event the trick is to be done impromptu.

91.   PAY DAY

"Pay Day" was introduced to magic by Tom Sellers. It is a commercial effect used by many magicians. In the following version, a borrowed $20 bill is sealed in an envelope. This envelope is mixed with two empty envelopes by a spectator.

Someone in the audience chooses one of the envelopes at random. This envelope is torn to pieces and thrown away. He then chooses another envelope. This envelope is also torn to pieces and thrown away.

Only one envelope remains. The spectator who lent the dollar bill is apprehensive that his bill was torn to shreds but, when the third envelope is opened, the borrowed bill is found safe inside.

Method: This handling is based on ideas suggested by Tom Harris and George Blake. Secretly place a pencil mark on one of the envelopes where you can easily spot it.

From a blank sheet of paper, cut out two dollar-size rectangles. Place one in each of the two unmarked envelopes and seal these envelopes. This completes the preparation.

Ask for the loan of a $20 bill. Have the spectator write his initials on the bill. Say, "That's so you'll recognize the bill in the event you ever see it again." Seal the bill in the envelope that has the pencil dot.

Hand all three envelopes to a spectator. Have him mix the envelopes until he is satisfied no one could possibly know the location of the envelope that contains the borrowed bill. Hand him a marking pen. Have him place a 1 on the front of one envelope, a 2 on another and a 3 on a third. Make sure he draws the numerals large enough to be clearly visible to the audience.

Have the spectator hold up the envelopes so the numbers can be seen by the audience. Ask the owner of the $20 bill to call out one of the numbers. Say he calls out No. 3.

Take envelope No. 3. Check to see if it has the secret pencil mark. If so, direct the spectator to tear up the remaining two envelopes. Then open envelope No. 3 to show that the borrowed bill is undamaged.

If envelope No. 3 does not have the pencil mark, tear it up and toss it aside. To increase the bill lender's anxiety, say, "I wish I had practiced this trick before attempting it."

After the envelope has been torn, say, "Of the remaining two envelopes, would you select one for me?"

The spectator might call out envelope No. 1. Take envelope No. 1. Check to see if it has the pencil mark. If it does, place it in the outer handkerchief pocket of your jacket, so that most of the envelope is clearly visible. It is logical to take the envelope and place it in your pocket because you asked the spectator to choose an envelope *for you.*

Have envelope No. 2 torn and thrown away. As this is done, say, "After all, it's only money." Let the tension build, then open envelope No. 1 to show that the borrowed bill is undamaged.

If envelope No. 1 does not have the pencil mark, tear it up and throw it away. Then have the remaining envelope opened and the borrowed bill returned to its owner.

92. SMART MONEY

The spectator removes a handful of change from his pocket. He chooses any coin and returns the other change to his pocket. The digits of the date on the chosen coin are multiplied together to arrive at a number. Then the number is reduced to a single digit.

The digit will be 9. The spectator opens *Self-Working Coin Magic* to the first page of any chapter and notes the ninth word in the opening sentence. That word will be "of." A previously written prediction is then opened to reveal that the magician correctly foretold that "of" would be chosen.

Method: This fine trick was invented by Sam Schwartz. Have the spectator choose a coin and note the date. Say the date is 1987. He multiplies the digits together to obtain $1 \times 9 \times 8 \times 7 = 504$.

The spectator then adds the digits in 504 together to obtain $5 + 0 + 4 = 9$. Unknown to the spectator, the date on any twentieth-century coin will reduce to the single digit 9 if the above procedure is used. The spectator can use a calculator to aid in the arithmetic.

Self-Working Coin Magic has been arranged so the ninth word in the opening sentence of any chapter is "of." The spectator can even open the book to the Introduction. Write the word "of" as a prediction, fold the paper and drop it into a drinking glass.

Have a word chosen by the above method. Let the spectator open the paper and verify that you correctly predicted the chosen word.

Sometimes the addition process will have to be used twice to reduce the number to a single digit. If the date on the coin is 1988, the spectator multiplies the digits together to obtain $1 \times 9 \times 8 \times 8 = 576$.

The spectator adds the digits in 576 to obtain $5 + 7 + 6 = 18$. Since this is not yet a single digit number, he adds the digits again to obtain $1 + 8 = 9$. The spectator then notes the ninth word of any chapter. The rest of the trick proceeds as described above.

A CATALOG OF SELECTED DOVER BOOKS IN ALL FIELDS OF INTEREST

CONCERNING THE SPIRITUAL IN ART, Wassily Kandinsky. Pioneering work by father of abstract art. Thoughts on color theory, nature of art. Analysis of earlier masters. 12 illustrations. 80pp. of text. 5⅜ x 8½. 23411-8

ANIMALS: 1,419 Copyright-Free Illustrations of Mammals, Birds, Fish, Insects, etc., Jim Harter (ed.). Clear wood engravings present, in extremely lifelike poses, over 1,000 species of animals. One of the most extensive pictorial sourcebooks of its kind. Captions. Index. 284pp. 9 x 12. 23766-4

CELTIC ART: The Methods of Construction, George Bain. Simple geometric techniques for making Celtic interlacements, spirals, Kells-type initials, animals, humans, etc. Over 500 illustrations. 160pp. 9 x 12. (Available in U.S. only.) 22923-8

AN ATLAS OF ANATOMY FOR ARTISTS, Fritz Schider. Most thorough reference work on art anatomy in the world. Hundreds of illustrations, including selections from works by Vesalius, Leonardo, Goya, Ingres, Michelangelo, others. 593 illustrations. 192pp. 7⅛ x 10¼. 20241-0

CELTIC HAND STROKE-BY-STROKE (Irish Half-Uncial from "The Book of Kells"): An Arthur Baker Calligraphy Manual, Arthur Baker. Complete guide to creating each letter of the alphabet in distinctive Celtic manner. Covers hand position, strokes, pens, inks, paper, more. Illustrated. 48pp. 8¼ x 11. 24336-2

EASY ORIGAMI, John Montroll. Charming collection of 32 projects (hat, cup, pelican, piano, swan, many more) specially designed for the novice origami hobbyist. Clearly illustrated easy-to-follow instructions insure that even beginning papercrafters will achieve successful results. 48pp. 8¼ x 11. 27298-2

THE COMPLETE BOOK OF BIRDHOUSE CONSTRUCTION FOR WOODWORKERS, Scott D. Campbell. Detailed instructions, illustrations, tables. Also data on bird habitat and instinct patterns. Bibliography. 3 tables. 63 illustrations in 15 figures. 48pp. 5¼ x 8½. 24407-5

BLOOMINGDALE'S ILLUSTRATED 1886 CATALOG: Fashions, Dry Goods and Housewares, Bloomingdale Brothers. Famed merchants' extremely rare catalog depicting about 1,700 products: clothing, housewares, firearms, dry goods, jewelry, more. Invaluable for dating, identifying vintage items. Also, copyright-free graphics for artists, designers. Co-published with Henry Ford Museum & Greenfield Village. 160pp. 8¼ x 11. 25780-0

HISTORIC COSTUME IN PICTURES, Braun & Schneider. Over 1,450 costumed figures in clearly detailed engravings—from dawn of civilization to end of 19th century. Captions. Many folk costumes. 256pp. 8⅜ x 11¾. 23150-X

STICKLEY CRAFTSMAN FURNITURE CATALOGS, Gustav Stickley and L. & J. G. Stickley. Beautiful, functional furniture in two authentic catalogs from 1910. 594 illustrations, including 277 photos, show settles, rockers, armchairs, reclining chairs, bookcases, desks, tables. 183pp. 6½ x 9¼. 23838-5

AMERICAN LOCOMOTIVES IN HISTORIC PHOTOGRAPHS: 1858 to 1949, Ron Ziel (ed.). A rare collection of 126 meticulously detailed official photographs, called "builder portraits," of American locomotives that majestically chronicle the rise of steam locomotive power in America. Introduction. Detailed captions. xi+ 129pp. 9 x 12. 27393-8

AMERICA'S LIGHTHOUSES: An Illustrated History, Francis Ross Holland, Jr. Delightfully written, profusely illustrated fact-filled survey of over 200 American lighthouses since 1716. History, anecdotes, technological advances, more. 240pp. 8 x 10¾. 25576-X

TOWARDS A NEW ARCHITECTURE, Le Corbusier. Pioneering manifesto by founder of "International School." Technical and aesthetic theories, views of industry, economics, relation of form to function, "mass-production split" and much more. Profusely illustrated. 320pp. 6⅛ x 9¼. (Available in U.S. only.) 25023-7

HOW THE OTHER HALF LIVES, Jacob Riis. Famous journalistic record, exposing poverty and degradation of New York slums around 1900, by major social reformer. 100 striking and influential photographs. 233pp. 10 x 7⅞. 22012-5

FRUIT KEY AND TWIG KEY TO TREES AND SHRUBS, William M. Harlow. One of the handiest and most widely used identification aids. Fruit key covers 120 deciduous and evergreen species; twig key 160 deciduous species. Easily used. Over 300 photographs. 126pp. 5⅜ x 8½. 20511-8

COMMON BIRD SONGS, Dr. Donald J. Borror. Songs of 60 most common U.S. birds: robins, sparrows, cardinals, bluejays, finches, more–arranged in order of increasing complexity. Up to 9 variations of songs of each species.
Cassette and manual 99911-4

ORCHIDS AS HOUSE PLANTS, Rebecca Tyson Northen. Grow cattleyas and many other kinds of orchids–in a window, in a case, or under artificial light. 63 illustrations. 148pp. 5⅜ x 8½. 23261-1

MONSTER MAZES, Dave Phillips. Masterful mazes at four levels of difficulty. Avoid deadly perils and evil creatures to find magical treasures. Solutions for all 32 exciting illustrated puzzles. 48pp. 8¼ x 11. 26005-4

MOZART'S DON GIOVANNI (DOVER OPERA LIBRETTO SERIES), Wolfgang Amadeus Mozart. Introduced and translated by Ellen H. Bleiler. Standard Italian libretto, with complete English translation. Convenient and thoroughly portable–an ideal companion for reading along with a recording or the performance itself. Introduction. List of characters. Plot summary. 121pp. 5¼ x 8½. 24944-1

TECHNICAL MANUAL AND DICTIONARY OF CLASSICAL BALLET, Gail Grant. Defines, explains, comments on steps, movements, poses and concepts. 15-page pictorial section. Basic book for student, viewer. 127pp. 5⅜ x 8½. 21843-0

THE CLARINET AND CLARINET PLAYING, David Pino. Lively, comprehensive work features suggestions about technique, musicianship, and musical interpretation, as well as guidelines for teaching, making your own reeds, and preparing for public performance. Includes an intriguing look at clarinet history. "A godsend," *The Clarinet,* Journal of the International Clarinet Society. Appendixes. 7 illus. 320pp. 5⅜ x 8½. 40270-3

THE ANNOTATED CASEY AT THE BAT: A Collection of Ballads about the Mighty Casey/Third, Revised Edition, Martin Gardner (ed.). Amusing sequels and parodies of one of America's best-loved poems: Casey's Revenge, Why Casey Whiffed, Casey's Sister at the Bat, others. 256pp. 5⅜ x 8½. 28598-7

THE RAVEN AND OTHER FAVORITE POEMS, Edgar Allan Poe. Over 40 of the author's most memorable poems: "The Bells," "Ulalume," "Israfel," "To Helen," "The Conqueror Worm," "Eldorado," "Annabel Lee," many more. Alphabetic lists of titles and first lines. 64pp. 5$\frac{3}{16}$ x 8¼. 26685-0

PERSONAL MEMOIRS OF U. S. GRANT, Ulysses Simpson Grant. Intelligent, deeply moving firsthand account of Civil War campaigns, considered by many the finest military memoirs ever written. Includes letters, historic photographs, maps and more. 528pp. 6⅛ x 9¼. 28587-1

ANCIENT EGYPTIAN MATERIALS AND INDUSTRIES, A. Lucas and J. Harris. Fascinating, comprehensive, thoroughly documented text describes this ancient civilization's vast resources and the processes that incorporated them in daily life, including the use of animal products, building materials, cosmetics, perfumes and incense, fibers, glazed ware, glass and its manufacture, materials used in the mummification process, and much more. 544pp. 6⅛ x 9¼. (Available in U.S. only.) 40446-3

RUSSIAN STORIES/RUSSKIE RASSKAZY: A Dual-Language Book, edited by Gleb Struve. Twelve tales by such masters as Chekhov, Tolstoy, Dostoevsky, Pushkin, others. Excellent word-for-word English translations on facing pages, plus teaching and study aids, Russian/English vocabulary, biographical/critical introductions, more. 416pp. 5⅜ x 8½. 26244-8

PHILADELPHIA THEN AND NOW: 60 Sites Photographed in the Past and Present, Kenneth Finkel and Susan Oyama. Rare photographs of City Hall, Logan Square, Independence Hall, Betsy Ross House, other landmarks juxtaposed with contemporary views. Captures changing face of historic city. Introduction. Captions. 128pp. 8¼ x 11. 25790-8

AIA ARCHITECTURAL GUIDE TO NASSAU AND SUFFOLK COUNTIES, LONG ISLAND, The American Institute of Architects, Long Island Chapter, and the Society for the Preservation of Long Island Antiquities. Comprehensive, well-researched and generously illustrated volume brings to life over three centuries of Long Island's great architectural heritage. More than 240 photographs with authoritative, extensively detailed captions. 176pp. 8¼ x 11. 26946-9

NORTH AMERICAN INDIAN LIFE: Customs and Traditions of 23 Tribes, Elsie Clews Parsons (ed.). 27 fictionalized essays by noted anthropologists examine religion, customs, government, additional facets of life among the Winnebago, Crow, Zuni, Eskimo, other tribes. 480pp. 6⅛ x 9¼. 27377-6

PERSPECTIVE FOR ARTISTS, Rex Vicat Cole. Depth, perspective of sky and sea, shadows, much more, not usually covered. 391 diagrams, 81 reproductions of drawings and paintings. 279pp. 5⅜ x 8½. 22487-2

DRAWING THE LIVING FIGURE, Joseph Sheppard. Innovative approach to artistic anatomy focuses on specifics of surface anatomy, rather than muscles and bones. Over 170 drawings of live models in front, back and side views, and in widely varying poses. Accompanying diagrams. 177 illustrations. Introduction. Index. 144pp. 8⅜ x11¼. 26723-7

GOTHIC AND OLD ENGLISH ALPHABETS: 100 Complete Fonts, Dan X. Solo. Add power, elegance to posters, signs, other graphics with 100 stunning copyright-free alphabets: Blackstone, Dolbey, Germania, 97 more—including many lower-case, numerals, punctuation marks. 104pp. 8⅛ x 11. 24695-7

HOW TO DO BEADWORK, Mary White. Fundamental book on craft from simple projects to five-bead chains and woven works. 106 illustrations. 142pp. 5⅜ x 8. 20697-1

THE BOOK OF WOOD CARVING, Charles Marshall Sayers. Finest book for beginners discusses fundamentals and offers 34 designs. "Absolutely first rate . . . well thought out and well executed."—E. J. Tangerman. 118pp. 7¾ x 10⅝. 23654-4

ILLUSTRATED CATALOG OF CIVIL WAR MILITARY GOODS: Union Army Weapons, Insignia, Uniform Accessories, and Other Equipment, Schuyler, Hartley, and Graham. Rare, profusely illustrated 1846 catalog includes Union Army uniform and dress regulations, arms and ammunition, coats, insignia, flags, swords, rifles, etc. 226 illustrations. 160pp. 9 x 12. 24939-5

WOMEN'S FASHIONS OF THE EARLY 1900s: An Unabridged Republication of "New York Fashions, 1909," National Cloak & Suit Co. Rare catalog of mail-order fashions documents women's and children's clothing styles shortly after the turn of the century. Captions offer full descriptions, prices. Invaluable resource for fashion, costume historians. Approximately 725 illustrations. 128pp. 8⅜ x 11¼. 27276-1

THE 1912 AND 1915 GUSTAV STICKLEY FURNITURE CATALOGS, Gustav Stickley. With over 200 detailed illustrations and descriptions, these two catalogs are essential reading and reference materials and identification guides for Stickley furniture. Captions cite materials, dimensions and prices. 112pp. 6½ x 9¼. 26676-1

EARLY AMERICAN LOCOMOTIVES, John H. White, Jr. Finest locomotive engravings from early 19th century: historical (1804–74), main-line (after 1870), special, foreign, etc. 147 plates. 142pp. 11⅜ x 8¼. 22772-3

THE TALL SHIPS OF TODAY IN PHOTOGRAPHS, Frank O. Braynard. Lavishly illustrated tribute to nearly 100 majestic contemporary sailing vessels: Amerigo Vespucci, Clearwater, Constitution, Eagle, Mayflower, Sea Cloud, Victory, many more. Authoritative captions provide statistics, background on each ship. 190 black-and-white photographs and illustrations. Introduction. 128pp. 8⅞ x 11¾. 27163-3

LITTLE BOOK OF EARLY AMERICAN CRAFTS AND TRADES, Peter Stockham (ed.). 1807 children's book explains crafts and trades: baker, hatter, cooper, potter, and many others. 23 copperplate illustrations. 140pp. 4⅝ x 6. 23336-7

VICTORIAN FASHIONS AND COSTUMES FROM HARPER'S BAZAR, 1867–1898, Stella Blum (ed.). Day costumes, evening wear, sports clothes, shoes, hats, other accessories in over 1,000 detailed engravings. 320pp. 9⅜ x 12¼. 22990-4

GUSTAV STICKLEY, THE CRAFTSMAN, Mary Ann Smith. Superb study surveys broad scope of Stickley's achievement, especially in architecture. Design philosophy, rise and fall of the Craftsman empire, descriptions and floor plans for many Craftsman houses, more. 86 black-and-white halftones. 31 line illustrations. Introduction 208pp. 6½ x 9¼. 27210-9

THE LONG ISLAND RAIL ROAD IN EARLY PHOTOGRAPHS, Ron Ziel. Over 220 rare photos, informative text document origin (1844) and development of rail service on Long Island. Vintage views of early trains, locomotives, stations, passengers, crews, much more. Captions. 8⅞ x 11¾. 26301-0

VOYAGE OF THE LIBERDADE, Joshua Slocum. Great 19th-century mariner's thrilling, first-hand account of the wreck of his ship off South America, the 35-foot boat he built from the wreckage, and its remarkable voyage home. 128pp. 5⅜ x 8½. 40022-0

TEN BOOKS ON ARCHITECTURE, Vitruvius. The most important book ever written on architecture. Early Roman aesthetics, technology, classical orders, site selection, all other aspects. Morgan translation. 331pp. 5⅜ x 8½. 20645-9

THE HUMAN FIGURE IN MOTION, Eadweard Muybridge. More than 4,500 stopped-action photos, in action series, showing undraped men, women, children jumping, lying down, throwing, sitting, wrestling, carrying, etc. 390pp. 7⅞ x 10⅝. 20204-6 Clothbd.

TREES OF THE EASTERN AND CENTRAL UNITED STATES AND CANADA, William M. Harlow. Best one-volume guide to 140 trees. Full descriptions, woodlore, range, etc. Over 600 illustrations. Handy size. 288pp. 4½ x 6⅜. 20395-6

SONGS OF WESTERN BIRDS, Dr. Donald J. Borror. Complete song and call repertoire of 60 western species, including flycatchers, juncoes, cactus wrens, many more–includes fully illustrated booklet. Cassette and manual 99913-0

GROWING AND USING HERBS AND SPICES, Milo Miloradovich. Versatile handbook provides all the information needed for cultivation and use of all the herbs and spices available in North America. 4 illustrations. Index. Glossary. 236pp. 5⅜ x 8½. 25058-X

BIG BOOK OF MAZES AND LABYRINTHS, Walter Shepherd. 50 mazes and labyrinths in all–classical, solid, ripple, and more–in one great volume. Perfect inexpensive puzzler for clever youngsters. Full solutions. 112pp. 8⅛ x 11. 22951-3

ANATOMY: A Complete Guide for Artists, Joseph Sheppard. A master of figure drawing shows artists how to render human anatomy convincingly. Over 460 illustrations. 224pp. 8⅜ x 11¼. 27279-6

MEDIEVAL CALLIGRAPHY: Its History and Technique, Marc Drogin. Spirited history, comprehensive instruction manual covers 13 styles (ca. 4th century through 15th). Excellent photographs; directions for duplicating medieval techniques with modern tools. 224pp. 8⅜ x 11¼. 26142-5

DRIED FLOWERS: How to Prepare Them, Sarah Whitlock and Martha Rankin. Complete instructions on how to use silica gel, meal and borax, perlite aggregate, sand and borax, glycerine and water to create attractive permanent flower arrangements. 12 illustrations. 32pp. 5⅜ x 8½. 21802-3

EASY-TO-MAKE BIRD FEEDERS FOR WOODWORKERS, Scott D. Campbell. Detailed, simple-to-use guide for designing, constructing, caring for and using feeders. Text, illustrations for 12 classic and contemporary designs. 96pp. 5⅜ x 8½. 25847-5

SCOTTISH WONDER TALES FROM MYTH AND LEGEND, Donald A. Mackenzie. 16 lively tales tell of giants rumbling down mountainsides, of a magic wand that turns stone pillars into warriors, of gods and goddesses, evil hags, powerful forces and more. 240pp. 5⅜ x 8½. 29677-6

THE HISTORY OF UNDERCLOTHES, C. Willett Cunnington and Phyllis Cunnington. Fascinating, well-documented survey covering six centuries of English undergarments, enhanced with over 100 illustrations: 12th-century laced-up bodice, footed long drawers (1795), 19th-century bustles, 19th-century corsets for men, Victorian "bust improvers," much more. 272pp. 5⅜ x 8¼. 27124-2

ARTS AND CRAFTS FURNITURE: The Complete Brooks Catalog of 1912, Brooks Manufacturing Co. Photos and detailed descriptions of more than 150 now very collectible furniture designs from the Arts and Crafts movement depict davenports, settees, buffets, desks, tables, chairs, bedsteads, dressers and more, all built of solid, quarter-sawed oak. Invaluable for students and enthusiasts of antiques, Americana and the decorative arts. 80pp. 6½ x 9¼. 27471-3

WILBUR AND ORVILLE: A Biography of the Wright Brothers, Fred Howard. Definitive, crisply written study tells the full story of the brothers' lives and work. A vividly written biography, unparalleled in scope and color, that also captures the spirit of an extraordinary era. 560pp. 6⅛ x 9¼. 40297-5

THE ARTS OF THE SAILOR: Knotting, Splicing and Ropework, Hervey Garrett Smith. Indispensable shipboard reference covers tools, basic knots and useful hitches; handsewing and canvas work, more. Over 100 illustrations. Delightful reading for sea lovers. 256pp. 5⅜ x 8½. 26440-8

FRANK LLOYD WRIGHT'S FALLINGWATER: The House and Its History, Second, Revised Edition, Donald Hoffmann. A total revision—both in text and illustrations—of the standard document on Fallingwater, the boldest, most personal architectural statement of Wright's mature years, updated with valuable new material from the recently opened Frank Lloyd Wright Archives. "Fascinating"—The New York Times. 116 illustrations. 128pp. 9¼ x 10¾. 27430-6

CATALOG OF DOVER BOOKS

AUTOBIOGRAPHY: The Story of My Experiments with Truth, Mohandas K. Gandhi. Boyhood, legal studies, purification, the growth of the Satyagraha (nonviolent protest) movement. Critical, inspiring work of the man responsible for the freedom of India. 480pp. 5⅜ x 8½. (Available in U.S. only.) 24593-4

CELTIC MYTHS AND LEGENDS, T. W. Rolleston. Masterful retelling of Irish and Welsh stories and tales. Cuchulain, King Arthur, Deirdre, the Grail, many more. First paperback edition. 58 full-page illustrations. 512pp. 5⅜ x 8½. 26507-2

THE PRINCIPLES OF PSYCHOLOGY, William James. Famous long course complete, unabridged. Stream of thought, time perception, memory, experimental methods; great work decades ahead of its time. 94 figures. 1,391pp. 5⅜ x 8½. 2-vol. set.
Vol. I: 20381-6   Vol. II: 20382-4

THE WORLD AS WILL AND REPRESENTATION, Arthur Schopenhauer. Definitive English translation of Schopenhauer's life work, correcting more than 1,000 errors, omissions in earlier translations. Translated by E. F. J. Payne. Total of 1,269pp. 5⅜ x 8½. 2-vol. set.
Vol. 1: 21761-2   Vol. 2: 21762-0

MAGIC AND MYSTERY IN TIBET, Madame Alexandra David-Neel. Experiences among lamas, magicians, sages, sorcerers, Bonpa wizards. A true psychic discovery. 32 illustrations. 321pp. 5⅜ x 8½. (Available in U.S. only.) 22682-4

THE EGYPTIAN BOOK OF THE DEAD, E. A. Wallis Budge. Complete reproduction of Ani's papyrus, finest ever found. Full hieroglyphic text, interlinear transliteration, word-for-word translation, smooth translation. 533pp. 6½ x 9¼. 21866-X

MATHEMATICS FOR THE NONMATHEMATICIAN, Morris Kline. Detailed, college-level treatment of mathematics in cultural and historical context, with numerous exercises. Recommended Reading Lists. Tables. Numerous figures. 641pp. 5⅜ x 8½. 24823-2

PROBABILISTIC METHODS IN THE THEORY OF STRUCTURES, Isaac Elishakoff. Well-written introduction covers the elements of the theory of probability from two or more random variables, the reliability of such multivariable structures, the theory of random function, Monte Carlo methods of treating problems incapable of exact solution, and more. Examples. 502pp. 5⅜ x 8½. 40691-1

THE RIME OF THE ANCIENT MARINER, Gustave Doré, S. T. Coleridge. Doré's finest work; 34 plates capture moods, subtleties of poem. Flawless full-size reproductions printed on facing pages with authoritative text of poem. "Beautiful. Simply beautiful."–Publisher's Weekly. 77pp. 9¼ x 12. 22305-1

NORTH AMERICAN INDIAN DESIGNS FOR ARTISTS AND CRAFTSPEOPLE, Eva Wilson. Over 360 authentic copyright-free designs adapted from Navajo blankets, Hopi pottery, Sioux buffalo hides, more. Geometrics, symbolic figures, plant and animal motifs, etc. 128pp. 8⅜ x 11. (Not for sale in the United Kingdom.) 25341-4

SCULPTURE: Principles and Practice, Louis Slobodkin. Step-by-step approach to clay, plaster, metals, stone; classical and modern. 253 drawings, photos. 255pp. 8⅛ x 11. 22960-2

THE INFLUENCE OF SEA POWER UPON HISTORY, 1660–1783, A. T. Mahan. Influential classic of naval history and tactics still used as text in war colleges. First paperback edition. 4 maps. 24 battle plans. 640pp. 5⅜ x 8½. 25509-3

THE STORY OF THE TITANIC AS TOLD BY ITS SURVIVORS, Jack Winocour (ed.). What it was really like. Panic, despair, shocking inefficiency, and a little heroism. More thrilling than any fictional account. 26 illustrations. 320pp. 5⅜ x 8½. 20610-6

FAIRY AND FOLK TALES OF THE IRISH PEASANTRY, William Butler Yeats (ed.). Treasury of 64 tales from the twilight world of Celtic myth and legend: "The Soul Cages," "The Kildare Pooka," "King O'Toole and his Goose," many more. Introduction and Notes by W. B. Yeats. 352pp. 5⅜ x 8½. 26941-8

BUDDHIST MAHAYANA TEXTS, E. B. Cowell and others (eds.). Superb, accurate translations of basic documents in Mahayana Buddhism, highly important in history of religions. The Buddha-karita of Asvaghosha, Larger Sukhavativyuha, more. 448pp. 5⅜ x 8½. 25552-2

ONE TWO THREE . . . INFINITY: Facts and Speculations of Science, George Gamow. Great physicist's fascinating, readable overview of contemporary science: number theory, relativity, fourth dimension, entropy, genes, atomic structure, much more. 128 illustrations. Index. 352pp. 5⅜ x 8½. 25664-2

EXPERIMENTATION AND MEASUREMENT, W. J. Youden. Introductory manual explains laws of measurement in simple terms and offers tips for achieving accuracy and minimizing errors. Mathematics of measurement, use of instruments, experimenting with machines. 1994 edition. Foreword. Preface. Introduction. Epilogue. Selected Readings. Glossary. Index. Tables and figures. 128pp. 5⅜ x 8½. 40451-X

DALÍ ON MODERN ART: The Cuckolds of Antiquated Modern Art, Salvador Dalí. Influential painter skewers modern art and its practitioners. Outrageous evaluations of Picasso, Cézanne, Turner, more. 15 renderings of paintings discussed. 44 calligraphic decorations by Dalí. 96pp. 5⅜ x 8½. (Available in U.S. only.) 29220-7

ANTIQUE PLAYING CARDS: A Pictorial History, Henry René D'Allemagne. Over 900 elaborate, decorative images from rare playing cards (14th–20th centuries): Bacchus, death, dancing dogs, hunting scenes, royal coats of arms, players cheating, much more. 96pp. 9¼ x 12¼. 29265-7

MAKING FURNITURE MASTERPIECES: 30 Projects with Measured Drawings, Franklin H. Gottshall. Step-by-step instructions, illustrations for constructing handsome, useful pieces, among them a Sheraton desk, Chippendale chair, Spanish desk, Queen Anne table and a William and Mary dressing mirror. 224pp. 8⅛ x 11¼. 29338-6

THE FOSSIL BOOK: A Record of Prehistoric Life, Patricia V. Rich et al. Profusely illustrated definitive guide covers everything from single-celled organisms and dinosaurs to birds and mammals and the interplay between climate and man. Over 1,500 illustrations. 760pp. 7½ x 10⅛. 29371-8

Paperbound unless otherwise indicated. Available at your book dealer, online at **www.doverpublications.com**, or by writing to Dept. GI, Dover Publications, Inc., 31 East 2nd Street, Mineola, NY 11501. For current price information or for free catalogues (please indicate field of interest), write to Dover Publications or log on to **www.doverpublications.com** and see every Dover book in print. Dover publishes more than 500 books each year on science, elementary and advanced mathematics, biology, music, art, literary history, social sciences, and other areas.